PRIMARILY
NEW HAMPSHIRE

A YEAR IN THE LIVES OF PRESIDENTIAL CAMPAIGN STAFFERS EXPLORED IN PHOTOGRAPHS & WORDS

BY MERYL LEVIN & WILL KANTERES

WITH FOREWORD BY ROBERT KERREY President, New School University

A THIRD RAIL PRESS BOOK

THIS PUBLICATION AND ACCOMPANYING EXHIBITION WERE MADE POSSIBLE IN PART BY GENEROUS SUPPORT FROM THE OFFICE OF THE PRESIDENT, NEW SCHOOL UNIVERSITY.

PUBLISHED BY **THIRD RAIL PRESS, INC**. PO BOX 356 NEW YORK, NY 10276 INFO@THIRDRAILPRESS.ORG WWW.THIRDRAILPRESS.ORG • ©2004 THIRD RAIL PRESS, INC. ALL RIGHTS RESERVED. • **PHOTOGRAPHS ©MERYL LEVIN COMMENTARY ©WILLIAM J. KANTERES FOREWORD ©ROBERT KERREY JOURNAL TEXT ©INDIVIDUAL STAFFERS, AS NOTED BELOW EACH TEXT. • DESIGN: JOHN FRANCIS PETERS PRINTED AND BOUND BY CJ GRAPHICS.** • LIBRARY OF CONGRESS CATALOG CARD NUMBER: 2003099722 ISBN: 0-9702744-1-6 • ALL PHOTOGRAPHS AND TEXTS WERE CREATED DURING THE 2003-2004 DEMOCRATIC PRESIDENTIAL PRIMARY SEASON IN NEW HAMPSHIRE. • NO PART OF THIS BOOK MAY BE USED OR REPRODUCED IN ANY MANNER WITHOUT WRITTEN PERMISSION FROM THE PUBLISHER.

INTRODUCTION: YOUR BACKSTAGE PASS

PIECING TOGETHER THE PHOTOS AND TEXT IN THIS BOOK WAS LIKE MAKING A MASSIVE MOSAIC.

We gathered the words of more than 30 campaign operatives and carefully overlaid them on the pictures that Meryl made during the year-long campaign. Our young collaborators held various positions on seven active New Hampshire campaign staffs. They shared many of the same experiences, so in some cases, the voice on the page does not belong to the person pictured there. A list of picture captions can be found at the back of the book. The pairings we created, and the pattern we assembled, are intended to make you feel more like a participant than an observer. The unrestricted access given to us by the campaigns, and the willingness of our participating staffers to generously share their thoughts and feelings, make this book better than a front-row ticket—it's your backstage pass.

The 2004 New Hampshire primary turned out to be spectacular political theater. When we began this project, we couldn't have imagined the drama that lay in store. In hindsight, there were plenty of signs: the number and caliber of the staffers, the money, the technology, the poignancy of the issues, and the spectrum of the candidates' personalities and ideologies. Add to that the most intensive media presence and scrutiny in New Hampshire primary history, and you have the ideal conditions for the political show of a lifetime.

Like the plot in a Broadway whodunit, this election was in a constant state of change—the frontrunner became the long shot, the insurgent became the frontrunner, and everyone in the middle fought for a moment in the spotlight. When the curtain finally came down, all but two were still on the stage, and the long shot was, once again, the frontrunner. The campaign staffers are the producers, writers, directors, set designers, and stagehands in this political production. When they do their jobs well, the audience doesn't notice them. They may feel exhausted and depleted as they exit the theater on opening night, but in fact, they are leaving enriched. The official results of any election are a permanent record of the vote count, but not of the tremendous personal growth, the lifetime friendships, and the emotional roller coaster that the staffers experience. The best way to get a sense of the electoral process is to read the words of those who've lived it. Their voices also help us understand campaign culture and why so many young people are drawn to it.

You may not be able kiss your family good-bye, put your mortgage on hold, and take a year sabbatical from your job to work on a campaign, but we hope this book will inspire you to affect change where you are and wield the privilege and power of your vote in every campaign. If you are young, in college, or starting a career, get in the habit of voting and don't miss the opportunity of a lifetime— working on a campaign.

—**Meryl Levin & Will Kanteres, April 2004**

FOREWORD

During one of the three Presidential debates in 2000 between Vice President Al Gore and Governor George W. Bush, a young man asked the candidates, "What are you going to do for young people?" Each answered with a short list of programs he hoped would please the audience. Both missed an opportunity to deflate a myth that politicians don't care what young Americans think by saying the simple and exciting truth: When it comes to campaigns and the governing that takes place after the elections, young people rule.

Young people rule because no candidate can succeed without them. No matter how much they depend upon television advertisements, direct mail, and, of late, the Internet, candidates simply cannot prevail unless they can convince hundreds, and sometimes thousands, of young men and women to voluntarily surrender their evenings, weekends, and vacations to help them.

Fortunately, plenty of young Americans are willing to do just that. And because they do, democracy survives. If they ever stop, our experiment in self-government might just do the same. By accepting participation in the democratic process as an integral part of citizenship as opposed to an elective activity, they demonstrate the value of weaving political action into daily life. We should be thankful that they have rejected the cynical advice of their elders who have turned away from freedom's highest calling after suffering a loss or disappointment. We should also let them inspire us to believe again that there is no "them" when it comes to serving our country or securing our democracy. There is only "us."

A political campaign—especially the exhilaration of a New Hampshire Presidential primary—is among the best peacetime life experiences. It is quite common for a college-age man or woman to be given responsibility and authority that far exceeds what they are likely to get any other way. The friendships created are of a kind that last a lifetime.

Most exciting for me is watching how many of the people who volunteer to campaign continue to serve in other ways. In the case of successful campaigns, these young volunteers often find themselves selected to do much of the heavy lifting in our state and nation's capitals. In part this is because they are the only ones with the energy to work the long hours required in elected offices.

Primarily New Hampshire gives us a glimpse of this youthful energy in motion. Look closely and you can see some of the powerful ideas that underlie democracy—the free and open debate of issues, the permission to carry those issues as far as possible, and the vital choice that each voter makes. It gives us a freeze-frame view of the techniques that accompany successful efforts—scheduling the candidate, canvassing a neighborhood, establishing visibility at events, and connecting with voters. It gives us a look at the commitment necessary for democracy to constantly re-create itself—including being prepared for the heartbreak of defeat.

Primarily New Hampshire also suggests things we can do to broaden participation. To increase racial, cultural, and economic diversity among campaign staff, our major parties should consider establishing discrete funds to be used to encourage and support young men and women who simply cannot join a campaign because the cost of travel alone is beyond their means.

As a beneficiary of volunteer workers in three successful statewide campaigns in Nebraska and one unsuccessful nationwide campaign, I can testify that watching young people grow into mature and capable democratic participants is the most satisfying part of public service. Young people managed every aspect of my campaigns. They followed me into office. They made friendships with each other and lasting friendships with me. The confidence earned from learning how to lead others cannot be gained in any classroom. The stories are the ones that we never stop retelling.

—**Robert Kerrey, President of New School University**
New York, April 2004

The price good men pay for indifference to public affairs is to be ruled by evil men.
—**Plato**

WAKE-UP CALL FOR DEMOCRACY

THE ALARM GOES OFF AT 5:30 AM. I LIFT MY HEAD OFF THE PILLOW, AND, IN THAT HALF ASLEEP/HALF AWAKE STATE OF CONSCIOUSNESS, MY IMMEDIATE REACTION IS TO ASK MYSELF: "IN WHICH HOTEL, WHICH CITY, AND WHICH CAMPAIGN AM I WAKING UP?"

As my senses sharpen, I realize that I'm at home, in my own bed and the only thing I have to advance is the dog's morning walk.

I'll admit it—I'm not naturally an early riser. Working on a campaign generates a mysterious, renewable energy that runs through your system and allows you to go from a dead sleep to 90 miles per hour in the time it takes the shower water to get hot. When you are on the road with a campaign, any predawn alarm in a dark room becomes the ignition switch for that energy source.

One of the few commodities each campaign shares equally is the number of days left until Election Day. You acquire a deeply engrained fear of oversleeping and screwing up one of those precious days. If you're five minutes late for the day's first event, that tardiness will grow exponentially until you're an hour late for the last event. Waiting in a hotel lobby—or worse, on a campaign bus—for half an hour at 6 am doesn't exactly put the press corps in the upbeat mood your press secretary strives for. And it doesn't matter if your candidate is a US senator sitting on the Transportation Committee—arriving at the gate even one minute late is too late for a scheduled airline flight. The list of threats, both real and imagined, goes on and on.

I'm afraid that Pavlovian power surge stays with you for the rest of your life. Early morning phone calls and alarm clocks, even a flight attendant call bell on a red-eye flight, will always trigger the campaign reveille response.

On this warm spring morning, the alarm tolls not for me, but for my partner Meryl. There is an early morning campaign event at a seniors' center in Peterborough, and she wants to get there in time to photograph the staff setting the stage for the candidate's appearance. Howard Dean speaking to seniors, John Kerry making his pitch to college students, John Edwards giving the keynote speech at a spaghetti dinner for Keene Dems, Bob Graham playing checkers with voters at historic Robie's Country Store, Dick Gephardt meeting and greeting old friends at a Dover house party (ah, the ubiquitous New Hampshire house parties!), Joe Lieberman delivering a pot of fresh coffee to firemen at a station house—these events will provide New Hampshire voters with the opportunity to piece together the platforms and personalities of those running for President.

LOOK THE CANDIDATES IN THE EYE, ASK ANY QUESTION, JUDGE THEIR HANDSHAKE, FIND OUT WHAT THEY STAND FOR POLITICALLY AND PERSONALLY, AND THEN CAST YOUR VOTE FOR THE LEADER OF THE FREE WORLD.

These countless venues are the settings for one of the most basic and essential functions in a direct democracy—knowing the essence of the candidate.

The more newsworthy events will be reported on and photographed by the national press and provide the rest of the world with a snapshot, often a lasting image, of the candidate's campaign. Not surprisingly, none of these moments happen without substantial effort. The time and energy expended on managing a successful, statewide campaign, and particularly on these events, are akin to mounting a military operation.

Every four years, dozens of political activists decide to give up a year of their lives to be a part of this democratic process. They eat, drink, and breathe politics for a year. Their birthdays pass uncelebrated; families are lucky if these foot soldiers of democracy show up for a couple of hours at holiday festivities. Relationships with friends who aren't political or who aren't registered to vote in New Hampshire are neglected. Who has time for novels or movies when you are constantly feeding your insatiable appetite for political news and world affairs from *The New York Times*, *The Washington Post*, CNN, *Roll Call*, *The*

Note, PoliticsNH.com, and Manchester's *Union Leader*?

These activists are the characters in the passion play we have chosen to explore. Their inspiration comes from varied sources. Their talents, techniques, and personalities cover a wide spectrum, yet they all share the same mission—to communicate their candidate's message, gather support from New Hampshire voters, deliver those voters to the polls, get the most votes. They are responsible for creating the infrastructure that enables us to perform our most elementary obligation as citizens of a republic. Society owes them a debt. If they are lucky enough to get their candidate elected, society repays them with the power to influence the policies of our federal government and the direction of our nation's future.

So, next time you pick up the *Times* and see a picture of a candidate standing in front of an American flag, flipping burgers for a group of National Guard troops, or reading a children's book to a group of 5-year-olds at the public library, somewhere in the background, just outside of the photographer's frame, is a 25-year-old campaign staff person/future Deputy Secretary of Whatever who created that particular moment.

—WILL KANTERES
Longtime political operative and New Hampshire native

We get the government we deserve.
—Don Henley, "A Month of Sundays," 1984

Arriving at the Manchester airport and taking a taxi to the hotel was jarring. **New Hampshire, and Manchester in particular, is full of campaign ghosts for me.** In 1996, as an Al Gore campaign field coordinator for the remote and rather bleak northern town of Berlin, I would relish the weekly meetings in Manchester to have human contact with my peers. I still count some of the '96 staffers as my closest friends. Seeing the mills, the familiar streets, the restaurants, I couldn't believe I was back, or how comfortable it felt.

I spent my first day driving around New Hampshire with Senator Lieberman, Joe Eyer (the political director of Lieberman's leadership PAC), and two other Lieberman staffers. I was uncertain of my role. As a field staffer, I would have hit up activists for volunteer support; as a political director, I would have worked the crowd, grabbing business cards; as a trip director, I would have had my eye on the clock to make sure everything was running on time. But I merely tagged along for the ride, just watching the show. Towards the end of a long day of campaigning, Eyer asked me how I thought it was going. He said that we would all have dinner that night and that I should be ready to give feedback to the senator. I was reminded of an early *West Wing* episode where Josh is convinced to go with candidate Bartlett to New Hampshire to see if the candidate "has what it takes."

That night at dinner I was almost giddy to be sitting at the table with a top-tier Presidential candidate, critiquing his performance and giving him my theory on how to win the New Hampshire primary. And like Josh, I was immediately smitten by the candidate. Throughout a long day he had impressed me (and the crowds) at each event with his knowledge, confidence, humor, and comfort with himself. Here was someone who wanted the job for the right reasons—because he believes that he could do better. A candidate with an inherently optimistic message: He believes that America is ready to elect a Jewish candidate, and his candidacy alone proves the greatness of the American people. And let's face it, who wouldn't want to feel like Josh on the *West Wing*?

And so I started working for Lieberman, first in the embryonic campaign headquarters on Massachusetts Avenue in DC, drawing up plans, outlining budget and staffing requirements, and placing calls to key New Hampshire pols. After a month in the cramped quarters, I was itching to get back to New Hampshire. I convinced the campaign that I was needed, now, on the ground in New Hampshire.

I packed my bags for a one-year stay, rented a car, and headed north.

—Peter Greenberger
NH State Director, Lieberman campaign

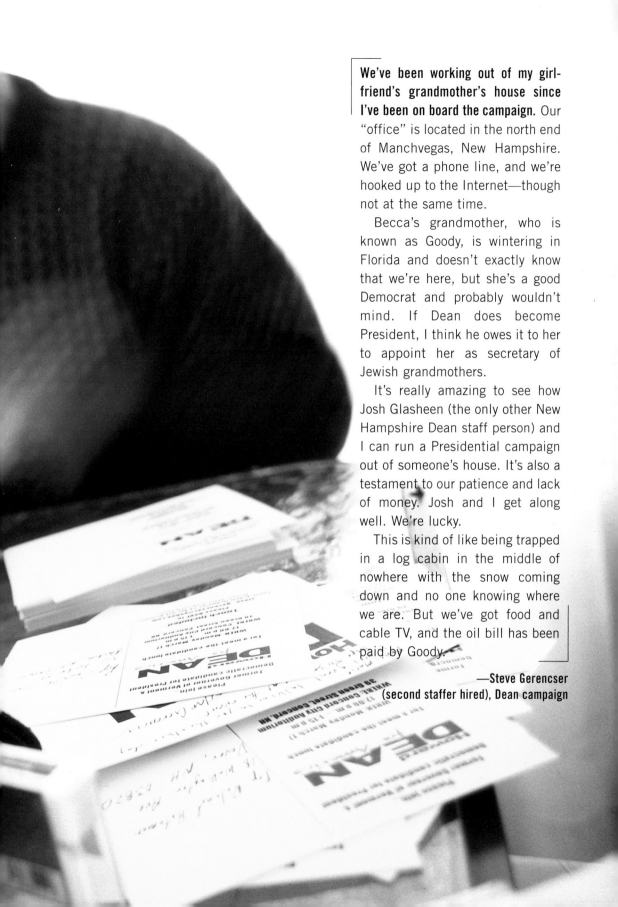

We've been working out of my girl-friend's grandmother's house since I've been on board the campaign. Our "office" is located in the north end of Manchvegas, New Hampshire. We've got a phone line, and we're hooked up to the Internet—though not at the same time.

Becca's grandmother, who is known as Goody, is wintering in Florida and doesn't exactly know that we're here, but she's a good Democrat and probably wouldn't mind. If Dean does become President, I think he owes it to her to appoint her as secretary of Jewish grandmothers.

It's really amazing to see how Josh Glasheen (the only other New Hampshire Dean staff person) and I can run a Presidential campaign out of someone's house. It's also a testament to our patience and lack of money. Josh and I get along well. We're lucky.

This is kind of like being trapped in a log cabin in the middle of nowhere with the snow coming down and no one knowing where we are. But we've got food and cable TV, and the oil bill has been paid by Goody.

—Steve Gerencser
(second staffer hired), Dean campaign

After Jeanne Shaheen's loss in the November 2002 New Hampshire senatorial election, the last thing I thought I would end up doing would be working on a Presidential campaign this cycle. In fact, I didn't read a newspaper for at least three weeks after the election—I certainly wasn't going to read one the day after the election because I couldn't imagine seeing headlines about Jeanne Shaheen and the analysis of the race.

Slowly but surely I started to revive my interest in politics. I got a call from a longtime supporter of Dick Gephardt asking if I had any interest in talking to

the Gephardt folks about working that campaign. Once I got into that mode, I figured, well, if I'm going to talk to Gephardt, I might as well start checking out a couple of other people. On my own, I initiated contact with Dean and Kerry people, and the more I thought about it, the more it seemed like it's what I wanted to do. And then John Kerry called me, and that was enough.

I also think, I hope I'm wrong, but I think it might be the last time New Hampshire has the first-in-the-nation primary—so what the heck, why not do it?

—Judy Reardon
Senior Advisor, Kerry campaign

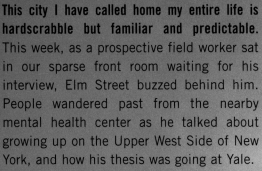

This city I have called home my entire life is hardscrabble but familiar and predictable. This week, as a prospective field worker sat in our sparse front room waiting for his interview, Elm Street buzzed behind him. People wandered past from the nearby mental health center as he talked about growing up on the Upper West Side of New York, and how his thesis was going at Yale.

The contrast between the street scene and this kid waiting for his interview was so striking. It really put into focus for me just how unpretentious and unglamorous the New Hampshire primary is. Despite the mythic status it has achieved, it's so far from the intellectual discourse on politics at college I heard last year, so far from the big money politics of New York and the West Coast, so far from the inside-the-Beltway power plays. Like the cityscape of Manchester out the office window, this process is raw and unadorned. It's not pretty, but it's basic—it's essential.

—Christopher Pappas
NH Deputy Field Director, Lieberman campaign

Only in New Hampshire can a young activist with just a few years' experience be hounded by each and every campaign, receive calls, letters, postcards from the candidate and members of his family and be lobbied by prominent state politicians from every angle. I quickly became desensitized to all the correspondence. I remember being nonplused one afternoon upon receiving a call from John Kerry himself, even as I was deciding whether I wanted to take a job on his campaign. I knew things were getting intimate when Mrs. Lieberman said in a message, "We NEED you on our team, honey."

—Christopher Pappas
NH Deputy Field Director, Lieberman campaign

The office is still far bigger than the number of people here, so we tend to communicate a lot over the phone (you **HAVE** to see these phones!), by instant messaging, and in traveling, impromptu meetings in each others' offices. My own space is in the corner, and if you crane your neck, there's a view of the old *Union Leader* building, where Ed Muskie cried during his infamous press conference in 1972. My own little piece of history.

—Colin Van Ostern
NH Press Secretary, Edwards campaign

Well, we moved into our new office and it's empty, dark, huge, and needs about 50 more people. We will no longer be using Goody's house. It's got a great view of downtown and feels much more Presidential than our previous digs.

I'm anxious to get things going. As of now I don't have any direct responsibility or position on the campaign and that of course is one of the biggest dangers of signing on early. When Josh and I signed on, all we had was a candidate—no state director, no office, no literature, NOTHING. But there are not many people who can say they were a part of a movement from the very beginning.

I believe you have to have as much faith in yourself as you do in your candidate. If you don't, you won't be able to see it through with the confidence that's needed to win or inspire others. Leadership is what makes the difference, and Dean offers that in a time when Democrats need it the most.

—Steve Gerencser
(later named) NH Deputy Political Director
Dean campaign

Never doubt that a small group of thoughtful, committed citizens can change the world; indeed it's the only thing that ever has.

—Margaret Mead

NEW HAMPSHIRE BIENVENUE

ONE OF THE FIRST THINGS YOU SEE UPON ENTERING NEW HAMPSHIRE IS A HUGE BILLBOARD THAT READS "NEW HAMPSHIRE BIENVENUE."

The sign was erected to encourage tourism by the state's Division of Travel & Tourism Development, but every four years it takes on a loftier message. During the Presidential primary, the "Welcome" sign is a greeting seemingly directed at an onslaught of campaign staffers, interns, consultants, journalists, pundits, weekend canvassers, and Presidential aspirants, all of whom must successfully negotiate this deadliest curve on the road to the White House.

For many Granite Staters, the warm welcome has nothing to do with hotel occupancy rates or Channel 9 media buys. It is about our desire to perform our democratic duty as citizens of this great republic. And we perform this duty with extreme diligence. We offer candidates the chance to talk to us, show us what they've got, and step under our microscope. In return, we welcome candidates and staff into our homes, feed them, inspect them (often more than once), learn from them, teach them, and accept or reject them during the year-long trial. On Election Night they sit back and watch the results of our intense scrutiny as our votes are tallied.

A great equalizer exists among New Hampshire residents. We share an unspoken awareness that, on Election Day, we all have equal power and equal wealth—our one vote. Getting that vote is the common goal of all candidates and their respective campaign teams during the Presidential primary.

Exit polls from the 2004 election tell us that 35 percent of New Hampshire voters decided how they would vote in the last three days. The other 65 percent spent weeks, or even months, making their decision. Voters like these do not rely solely on newspapers and television to make their choice—they demand face time. As a result, a good deal of campaign time and effort in the year leading up to Election Day is spent reaching out to these conscientious voters.

The campaign organizers who have experienced this process before know what needs to be done. New Hampshire voters want to determine the candidates' character before they become involved in their campaign, and the best way for them to do that is to see the candidate in action under various battlefield conditions.

Love at first sight is a rare occurrence in the New Hampshire primary. Most respectable New Hampshire voters want more than one dance before they commit to their political "hookup." Proper voters need a courting phase to make sure they choose the right candidate. They want to know all about his or her past record, present policies, and vision of America's future. Some may even be seen at two or three events for a candidate in a 24-hour period. They want to see what a candidate is like offstage as well as on. They want to meet a candidate's family and introduce him or her to their own friends and family. Only then will the professional New Hampshire voter pledge his or her undying (in most cases) support.

In an era where 50 percent of marriages end in divorce, it comes as no surprise that a New Hampshire activist will occasionally rescind his or her endorsement. This behavior is rare and, more often than not, is the result of "high maintenance" activists who feel that the campaign is not incorporating their advice or is neglecting them in some manner. Nick Clemons, New Hampshire field organizer extraordinaire, claims to have coined the perfect name for such supporters: "Jacktivists."

A classic example is the report (or is it an urban myth?) of the alderman who had reluctantly given an early endorsement to a promising candidate in a crowded field. According to a staffer in that campaign, the alderman agreed to accompany the candidate on a traditional downtown walk to meet and greet local merchants. Upon entering a small sweet shop, the candidate instinctively purchased a dozen cookies. Well, he should have asked for a baker's dozen because just as he turned to offer the alderman a cookie, he realized the bag was empty—a minor offense in geo-political terms, but serious enough to prompt the alderman to withdraw his endorsement the next day.

Perhaps that highway sign should read, "New Hampshire Bienvenue, entrez à vos risques et périls."

WILL KANTERES

We were met at the West Lebanon, New Hampshire, airport by a lone student and driven the several miles into Hanover in an ancient, semi-enclosed Jeep with the next Presidential nominee of the Democratic Party in the front seat and his future campaign manager rattling around on top of the luggage. Somehow this did not conform to my preconceptions of a Presidential campaign. . . . [W]here were the limousines?

—Gary Hart, *Right From the Start*, 1973

The most obvious difference about this job and most other professions is the transient lifestyle. While most of my college friends have lived in one or two cities since graduation, I have lived in nine cities (a few more than once), in countless apartments and homes.

When you move so much, you never have the chance to establish any sense of permanence anywhere—or to pick up much in the way of property or belongings. I never bought an apartment in DC, so the bulk of my stuff still sits in boxes at my parents' house. I have no need to store furniture; I've never bought anything worth storing. The purchases that I make are always on the fly and serve only to fill an immediate need. I expect to discard everything at the end of the campaign. Cars are a perfect example.

I drove a lemon rental in '96 that broke down in northern New Hampshire, an area called the Notch. It was after midnight; temperatures were 20 degrees below. I was driving home after a Friday meeting when the lights began to dim and the wipers started moving very slowly. Roads in the Notch have no shoulder and it snows there perpetually. I turned off the radio and contemplated turning off my headlights to

preserve enough power to make it out the other side. The car died a few yards outside of the Notch. Luckily, a man in an SUV came by and gave me a ride. This was my first hitchhiking experience, and I remember being a little nervous getting into the car. But after a few minutes my field instincts took over and though I failed to get him to sign a steering committee form, he did promise to consider voting for Bill Clinton.

This time, once again, I drove to New Hampshire in a rental, assuming that I would find a vehicle after I settled in. A local supporter followed me to the airport where we dropped off the rental car and made our way to a dealership. It was 10 am. I told the salesman that I needed a car in a hurry; after all, I had a 12 pm lunch meeting. Perhaps not the greatest negotiation strategy, but I did manage to get a very good deal on an American car, arrange for insurance, and sign all the necessary paperwork in record time.

I was on the road when I got a call from HQ in DC. "I just bought a car," I announced. They asked the next logical question, "What kind?" There was a pause on my end of the phone. "Uh . . . not really sure. It's white and I think a Chevrolet. Hold on a minute." I put the phone down and grabbed the owner's manual from the glove compartment. "Looks like a 2001 Chevy Metro." So far, the car has been perfect. I may even keep this one.

—Peter Greenberger
NH State Director, Lieberman campaign

My previous boss, Kathy Sullivan (chair of the New Hampshire Democratic Party), likened February 2003 to high-school graduation—everyone setting off on their own, in a different direction. It feels a bit more like a college draft to me—since we all know we're setting off for opposing teams. Guessing when we all stop talking to each other is a running joke. For a few people, it probably isn't a joke.

At dinner the other night, Al Sharpton shot back at those saying he didn't have a chance to win: "I have news for you. Eight of us are running. Seven are going to lose." And so, each of us is setting off on a job where chances are we'll be with one of those seven losers. I suppose it won't hurt to have friends on all the other campaigns in a year when one of us is going to be fielding a lot of calls from job seekers. Of course, we're all firmly convinced that we'll be on the receiving end of those calls.

—Colin Van Ostern
NH Press Secretary, Edwards campaign

At first I found it a bit awkward coming into the New Hampshire scene because it was all so new to me. But I have found my niche, and I love the people that I have been working with. I like the quaint New England feel. I like running around the residential areas in the morning, taking in the town as most people are sleeping, trying to view it all as a resident, not as someone who has descended here to identify voting patterns and behaviors among Democrats and Independents. I think to myself that these poor people don't know what will hit them in just a couple of months, even those who have gone through it before.

—Johanna Voss
Statewide Volunteer/Intern Coordinator, Kerry campaign

Running an event is like cooking. You have to have a sense in advance of what the ingredients are, what has to be done, how long each step will take, and what the final product is supposed to look like.

You have to be able to do several things at the same time—keep reporters abreast of what will happen, make sure the visual is laid out right, make sure the participants are in the right spot. Then you have to be able to monitor everything, that is, make sure nothing is burning (too small of a crowd, an embarrassing backdrop, a late-breaking story that one reporter is working on). And like any good cook, you have to taste along the way, adding a bit more here or there, prompting a question, bringing the event to a close.

Also like cooking, the hardest part is usually timing. Far too often, it's (past) time to go, and no one wants to leave. Edwards wants to keep taking questions, the audience wants to keep asking them, the reporters want to grab him by the door, and meanwhile another event on the other side of town is supposed to start right about NOW. You do your best to plan the times right in advance, but you end up slightly off, and you struggle to make sure the steak is ready at the same time the side dish is warm.

—Colin Van Ostern
NH Press Secretary, Edwards campaign

Our new office is abuzz with activity. We now have five full-time regional field organizers, along with two deputy field directors. This weekend is our first big field activity, a statewide canvass. So the field staff is hustling to pull together walk lists, cut maps, and, of course, prepare contingency plans for the inevitable rain showers that will no doubt curtail some of our canvass.

While I'm glad to be in an office and close to the rest of the staff, part of me will miss working from home. The fact that I did not have a commute for nearly five months was great, something I've never experienced before. There is definitely something to be said for doing your work in pajamas. Also, I'll miss being able to spend so much time with my wife.

The long march has begun in earnest....

—Nick Clemons
NH Field Director, Kerry campaign

	Chair	Town	Chair	Town
...rd		Dorchester		
...water		Dublin		
...tol		Dummer		
...kline		Dunbarton		
...bridge		Easton		
...npton		Ellsworth		
...naan		Enfield		
...nterbury		Errol		
...arroll		Fitzwilliam		
...arlestown		Francestown		
...estefield		Franconia		
		Franklin		
		Gilsum		

Sometimes, as I walk the streets of Nashua, I feel as if I, as if we, the politicos, are the only ones out there, all alone, going door-to-door. I know enough to not expect a warm welcome—I canvassed for several campaigns in Missouri, when I was in college. But something about this election (Presidential) and this state (New Hampshire) led me to believe that maybe, just maybe, folks would be excited.

For the most part, the doors I knock on are answered by average citizens, no more or less engaged than my parents. "It's awfully early," many begin. And not because they don't like my candidate, but because they don't particularly like politics, the pursuit of power. But when I get into my spiel—Dean balanced the budget 11 years straight in Vermont; health care for virtually

all children and 92 percent of adults, etc.—they get interested. They start criticizing Bush, embracing the Doctor.

The early evening is already my favorite time of day to canvass. I'm three-quarters of the way into my shift. I've signed up a supporter or two, converted an ex-Kerry backer, got a couple doors slammed in my face—the whole range of responses. Invariably, I get a second wind, talking to a young voter I persuade to register, or learning about how a single mom without health insurance is getting by.

As I walk by the apple orchard, the sun sets. A beautiful scene. The sky is a million shades of red, pink, blue. But all is quiet. And I keep walking.

—Yoni Cohen
(later named) Salem/Derry Regional Field Director, Dean Campaign

Choosing a candidate is a bit like being set up on a blind date. Before I decided to work for Dean, I'd met him a few times, had a few conversations with him, read everything I could about him, and talked to people who know and have worked for him. I knew that our politics were similar enough, and temperamentally he seemed okay, as best I could tell. But there were all these other things about him that were totally unknown to me. It's like when a friend has a friend who might be a good match for you. When they set you up, they describe the person in the broadest of brushstrokes. Missing, though, are all of the essential particulars—things revealed with time, the small, unlikely things that make or break relationships. How does he treat waitresses? Is he nice to his mother?

About a month after I signed on, Governor Dean spoke to a class at Saint Anselm College in Manchester. In the Q & A, a guy asked a pointed question about special education and commented that kids with disabilities generally dumb down classes and force everyone to slow down. My stomach lurched. I've got deep ties to the disability-rights movement in New Hampshire and have done a lot of organizing to support the full inclusion of people with disabilities in schools, communities, and the workplace. It was a question that mattered, and if he didn't get it right, it would be very uncomfortable for me. It's possible to coach a candidate on certain kinds of answers to questions, but it's impossible to coach someone into having different values.

In responding, Dean began with part of his standard stump—the need to make the federal government live up to its obligation to fully fund special education. The guy who asked the question then said that it's not just about money. Having those kids in the classroom slows everyone else down. It takes away from the "normal" kids in the classroom, he maintained. Dean disagreed and then spoke about the experience of his own children (Vermont has the highest rate of inclusion of kids with disabilities in the country). First, he said, having kids with disabilities means more adults in the classroom and no kid, regardless of his or her challenges, needs an aide full-time, so the aide is available to assist other students. Second, Dean said, inclusion is not just good for kids with disabilities, which it is, it's good for all kids. His son Paul benefited from developing friendships with kids of differing abilities, and that's what public education is all about.

My stomach went back to normal. It was a perfect answer. I knew we would get to a second date.

—Karen Hicks
NH State Director, Dean campaign

The world is moved along, not only by the mighty shoves of its heroes,
but also by the aggregate of the tiny pushes of each honest worker.
—Helen Keller

LONESOME COWBOYS & COWGIRLS

AS THE MOMENTUM OF THE CAMPAIGN BUILDS, IT IS INEVITABLE THAT ALL OF THOSE INVOLVED IN IT WILL GET PULLED ALONG BY THE ENERGY IT CREATES.

The campaign becomes as powerful as a force of nature. When you're a staffer in the early stages of a campaign, you may notice aspects of everyday life that are no longer part of your daily routine. Then, when things start cranking, you become so focused that you lose sight of the universe that exists beyond the campaign world. Some days are so hectic that you find yourself making decisions and taking actions without the benefit of extended analysis or the counsel of your co-workers. The number of decisions you must make or issues you must respond to come at you with such velocity that you are forced to go with a "no huddle" offense—trusting your gut instincts and making snap decisions on the run. Certainly, there is not enough time to worry about whether you're current on your car payments or if it's time for you to see a doctor about that shooting pain in your lower back.

So, one minute you're facing the full force of a Category 5 hurricane, and then, every once in a while, the strangest thing happens. I can only describe it as the opposite of an out-of-body experience. You are backstage at an event, or in the middle of a crowd, or in a private meeting, when all of a sudden you notice a sense of calm, and you become intensely aware of yourself and your surroundings. You start to realize that everything you have been doing for the entire day, possibly the entire week, has been like the autopilot response of a 737 going through turbulence. You briefly regain your personal identity and start to think about how much you miss your loved ones and that maybe you should just call and tell someone you love them. Your senses come alive, and you start to notice every detail of your environment—like a newborn in a delivery room opening its eyes for the first time.

Then the lonesome cowboy blues start to creep in. The sudden awareness of who you are and where you are brings with it a sense of guilt and loneliness. Just as you start to feel bad for yourself, the eye of the storm passes. You get lifted off the ground and twisted around by the next crisis. The last thing you remember thinking about is how you're going to deal with these feelings on the day after the election.

WILL KANTERES

To some extent, I think that those of us who worked on Jeanne Shaheen's New Hampshire US Senate campaign last year learned what happens when you get over-invested in this line of work. It took me so long to get over last campaign's loss. It was as if I was wounded. It's kind of like falling in love for the first time. When that love ends, you get hurt, and you never let yourself fall in love that deeply again. And that's how it is with the candidate. I love what I do for Howard Dean and I love what he stands for, but I do not have that googly-eyed love that I had for Jeanne Shaheen.

I have to keep myself at this level of reality about this election for my own well-being. I feel that if I don't remind myself of that all the time, I'm going to have another two months after all this of giving up hope on the American people in general and what I've chosen to do with my life.

—Delana Jones
Manchester Regional Field Director, Dean campaign

The campaign organization is like a zygote. In the early stages after the fertilization, all the cells do the exact same thing. Then as the egg matures, there is very fast growth and cells specialize.

Everyone on the campaign is doing the same thing—we have no specialists, except me. My specialty is answering questions and solving problems. The problems keep coming. It's just like a Kleenex box—you solve one problem, and another one pops up in its place. Slowly, we are starting to get systems into place, and I can step back and think, "OK, where is the breakdown happening; how can we address this systemically?" Once you step away from being in the weeds, you start to see patterns emerging. I need to see those patterns and not spend my time trying to dig out of a hole, solving problem after problem.

—Karen Hicks
NH State Director, Dean campaign

My family, although very supportive, is utterly confused about the career choices I have made. When I decided to move to New Hampshire and work on a Presidential campaign, they were less than excited. The idea of taking a job with absolutely no job security was very frightening for them. To be totally honest, it was more than a little frightening for me as well.

The question then became, "Why do it?" The answer I kept coming back to was, "How could I not?" The opportunity to have a role in electing the next President of the United States is not one that comes around every day and is not one I could refuse. No matter how many long hours would be required, no matter how little money would be involved, no matter that my friends and family thought I was nuts—I had no option. I was drawn to the campaign and campaign life.

—Kristina Saunders
NH Deputy Press Secretary, Graham campaign

I think that a certain culture definitely begins to take shape on a campaign. It's interesting because right now, we're one happy family. Everyone from the state director down to the interns knows one another and talks on a daily basis. However, soon enough we're going to see a social division similar to that of a military hierarchy.

The field staffers, average age of about 24, are the privates. They won't fraternize with Ken Robinson [state director] or Judy Reardon [senior advisor]. The field director deputies are like sergeants—they lead two squads of field staffers. I'm like a captain—I oversee the field deputies but will have increasingly less and less interaction with the field staffers. And Ken is the general, overseeing not only the field staff but also the other divisions of press and politics, each of which will have their own hierarchy.

—Nick Clemons
NH Field Director, Kerry campaign

Our first canvass was the same day as the memorial service for Peg Dobbie, longtime executive director of NARAL-NH and a supreme grassroots organizer. I'd felt a little bad when the canvass was scheduled for that day, wondering if it was disrespectful to Peg. But her memorial service was, in part, a celebration of her commitment to grassroots organizing. So while at the service, which was beautiful, I decided Peg wouldn't mind that folks were going door-to-door for a cause they believed in on this day.

—Judy Reardon
Senior Advisor, Kerry campaign

New Hampshire is a one-voter-at-a-time state. Most activists will say that they're unwilling to commit to candidates until they meet them. To a lot of people outside of New Hampshire, this sounds outrageous, given that most Americans' exposure to politics is through 30-second TV ads.

That said, going door-to-door is a great way to pique someone's interest about a candidate. It allows us to talk about John Kerry conversationally with voters, giving us a chance to answer any questions they may have about his record. Generally we ask the voters about issues that concern them and usually end our conversations by inviting the voters to come see Kerry at an event.

—Nick Clemons
NH Field Director, Kerry campaign

One of the most challenging aspects of my job is building a team that can win. It sounds ridiculously simplistic and, in a way, it is. The staff people that we're attracting are smart, energetic, totally committed, and really, really, really young. For most of them, this is their first "real" job—a few have worked on campaigns before. How do we take this raw energy and brilliance and turn it into a team that is more than the sum of the parts and gets better over time? All of these staffers will learn on their own—mostly from practice and by making mistakes—but we need to figure out how to accelerate that learning.

To help build the foundation for learning, I'm trying to be very deliberate about the culture of our organization. Each campaign has a culture— deliberately or not—so we may as well be explicit about how we are going to work together. Last weekend, we had a retreat for staff and key supporters where we agreed on five values we needed to share to work together effectively. Going in, I think some people were a little nervous and had been practicing renditions of *Kumbaya*, but once we started, everybody dug in. We decided on the following: results orientation to keep everyone focused on the 60,000 votes we need to identify and turn out on Election Day; accountability, meaning taking real responsibility for getting things done; honesty to help with learning, and to help me provide the right kind of support to get to the outcome we want; loyalty—to Howard Dean and the team—to keep us from being divided when things get rough; and resiliency to help us recover from the inevitable bumps in the road—and of course, to learn from them.

The other thing that will be hard will be keeping people motivated. Campaigns, even the biggest, most exciting ones, are made up a series of mundane steps that are the necessary work of winning. What the hell does addressing postcard invitations have to do with taking our country back? Everything. The care, approach, and energy that we put into these mundane steps will determine our success. A friend of mine gave me this great analogy: You're walking down the street, and you see this person mixing concrete and you say, "Hey, what are you doing?" He says, "I'm mixing concrete." And you say, "Oh, OK," and walk on. Further down the road, there is another guy who is really enthusiastically mixing concrete, and you say, "Hey, what are you doing?" And he says, "I'm building a cathedral." We have to help people understand that writing postcards, making phone calls, and going door-to-door is building the cathedral of change we need in politics.

—Karen Hicks
NH State Director, Dean campaign

"Field work," in a nutshell, is an organizing tool used to build relationships with people. So we start by forming lists of people who have been active in the past. Then we start asking ourselves questions: How can we get these people engaged; to what degree are they usually engaged; and what can they produce for the campaign? We pick out key volunteers, or "Dean Leaders," as we call them. We get to know them, and know what they can give you, and create teams of people based on their strengths.

As Manchester field director, I'm responsible for 23 percent of the votes we need to win the campaign, about 11,000 votes. It's about looking at where you want to be on Election Day and then walking backwards. Well, obviously I can't reach 11,000 people myself, so I need people engaging other people. I need this many doors to be knocked on; I need this many people identified. It's just planning. The whole challenge from now until Election Day is how are we going to get there.

We knocked on over 3,000 doors, just in Manchester. Our team averaged 200-300 houses a person, per day. And we got a 21 percent contact rate, meaning that's how many voters were at home and would talk to us. When you do the math, you quickly realize you have to start thinking of other ways to reach people. So I created a script for "chase calls," and I'll get other people to make the calls and say, "You know the Dean campaign left some literature at your door last week. Did you have a chance to read it? Do you have any questions? Do you need any more information?" Then we try to ID them on the phone. This will happen in every region. Just last April I had no idea how to do this. I learned while doing it back then, when I worked on Jeanne Shaheen's Senate race.

—Delana Jones
Manchester Regional Field Director, Dean campaign

The first week was exciting, scary, exhilarating, and overwhelming all at once. I definitely have new-job disorientation, e.g.: "Is there any water around here?" "Jessie, I forgot my three new passwords, again." "Yeah, I didn't get that e-mail about the meeting I just missed." "Is it always this dusty in here?"

Monday: Ken Robinson called me at 6:30 am to make sure I was up and ready for our drive to Conway at 7. I was in the shower and didn't answer the phone. I am sure for a split second that he thought I was dead asleep. Drove to Conway going about 85 miles an hour because we were late. Ken probably wished I was going 95, but since I was driving without my glasses I thought it best to be safe. (If you are wondering, my glasses fell casualty underneath my TV during the move in.) Kerry was late; he had not seen his speech; there was spotty cell-phone reception—your basic nightmare. We winged it. Went fine. Kerry was good in the hall and great in the private meeting.

Tuesday: Got to the office around 8:20 am. By 10, I was in meetings that I was not aware of beforehand. Break for lunch with Ken and Nick. Back to meetings until 2:30, at which point I had to have the meetings that I had originally scheduled but had to cancel due to the meetings I hadn't known about. At 4:30 sat down to do work for the first time since 10 am. Panic set in. I have way too much shit to do and it is only June . . . fuuuucccckkkk.

Wednesday: Uneventful. Just work.

Thursday: More work. Great veterans meeting at 7 pm, went for over three hours. Four guys who have been with Kerry for almost 30 years came to talk to New Hampshire folks. It was amazing. Home at midnight. Again, only June.

—Theo Yedinsky
NH Political Director, Kerry campaign

I'm having trouble allowing people to make mistakes. It's how I learn. It's how everyone learns, but it feels like we're in a high-stakes fish bowl with so many people watching. Judging. It's also hard because I don't know the team well yet—who you can count on and who needs more help. I also do not know how they will do it—will they worry about things enough? I want people who will worry, worry, worry about everything.

I know this is part of the difficult transition for me, from doing to managing. That's what's been waking me up at three in the morning. So what I've started doing the last few days is getting up at 5:30 am and taking two hours to think

only in broad strokes, longer term. It's hard to have the discipline to focus beyond the end of your nose because we're swimming among all of these little things that have to happen. My automatic inclination is to jump up, turn on the computer, and start sending out e-mails about the immediate thing TODAY, rather than think about the voter contact plan. Then, from 7:30 to 9:30, I respond to the e-mails from the previous day. By 9:30 the phone really starts to ring, and from then on I'm pretty much on the phone all day long.

—Karen Hicks
NH State Director, Dean campaign

I'm certainly mastering the art of office cooking—tonight's dinner is broccoli and a sweet potato that I cooked in an old microwave passed down from a previous Senate campaign. I just checked my voice mail, which was full of messages from my friends back in Boston with "normal" jobs—the ones that end at 5. I often find myself thinking what it must be like to have a job like that. Sometimes, I think it must be great—weeknights and weekends to do whatever you want, vacation time, personal days. In this job it's hard to get a personal hour.

Working on a campaign can definitely put rifts in your relationships—particularly with people who are not interested in politics. I'm getting frustrated with friends who don't seem to care or know anything about the election or dismiss it and what I'm doing with comments like, "Why do you work so hard and care so much—he's not going to win anyway." I really do love what I'm doing. I don't think I could work a 9-to-5 anyway. What would I do from 5 until I go to bed? Probably just watch *Crossfire* and *Hardball*—I think it's definitely better to be living politics instead of just watching it on TV!

—Emily Silver
NH Deputy State Director & Chief of Staff, Lieberman campaign

I am sick. I've been sneezing my head off for 48 hours. I think part of it is the pollen, and part of it is just the intensity of the job. This past week, in particular, was pretty hectic. We had Lieberman's wife, Hadassah (or "H" as we like to call her), in New Hampshire on Tuesday and Wednesday and our national campaign manager, Craig Smith, in town on Thursday and Friday.

With H we traveled the state, starting in Manchester and ending up in Lyme. She was great and seems to have a way with people. I think H is at her best when she is telling personal stories that are close to her heart—people respond to that sort of warmth and sincerity.

The trip also provided me with a needed injection of "real people." As press secretary on the campaign, I work all the time in front of a computer screen, read newspaper after newspaper, talk only to political reporters and other political wonks, and spend any free time with all the same people. It's nice to break out every now and then and talk to people who are far from this campaign world.

I don't think I've ever had more caffeine than I did over the three days H and Craig were here. With H, we stopped in diner after diner, and with Craig we met five reporters at five different coffee shops. I ordered a cup of coffee at each stop; hence, I was completely and utterly wired by 1 pm and just crashed hard, hard, hard around 3. Not so good for the body. The nonstop sneezing, runny nose, itchy eyes, and headache started Thursday afternoon.

As far as Manchester goes, I'm settling in, though I miss New York and my friends there quite a bit. I haven't been back since I moved here—I was supposed to go last weekend but canceled at the last minute. I knew I wouldn't be able to relax because the week ahead would have been constantly on my mind—I would've been physically there but mentally here. This, of course, would have thoroughly annoyed my friends (I'm already on thin ice with many of them for "disappearing"). On top of that, I would have suffered from the classic campaign guilt of not being in the office—that guilt of not being there when there is so, so much to do. How could I go off for an entire weekend and have fun, when I go home every day feeling like I didn't get through half of the work I wanted to? I have promised myself that I will not let that damned guilt rule my life over the next eight months, but I must admit, this requires a daily pep talk with myself, and often the pep talk is not effective.

—Kristin Carvell
NH Press Secretary, Lieberman campaign

[P]olitics, an art more readily acquired by association than by study.
—James F. Byrnes, former governor of South Carolina,
Senator, Supreme Court Justice

Observing the young organizers working together, or in some cases against each other, brings to mind Yogi Berra's famous line, "It's déjà vu all over again." I feel like I've met most of them before, but they had different names and were working for different candidates. When I walk into the various campaign headquarters, I can't help picturing the faces of my own friends from past campaigns. To this day, those friends are never more than a phone call away. Although the young campaign staffers are too busy to think about their personal futures, I'm struck by a strange confluence of nostalgia and prescience that gives me a unique vision of what is in store for this new generation of organizers.

Campaign work was the first step for many of my friends on the path to substantial achievements: first woman elected governor of New Hampshire, youngest mayor of a major city, senior partner in one of the country's most respected public-policy firms, founder of a leading hunger-relief organization, and senior advisors to Presidents.

Today's staffers are traveling the same road. The 22-year-old advance person sharing a desk with the 25-year-old press secretary may share a meal one day as a US senator and a network news anchor. The 19-year-old intern driving the candidate's van may someday lead a convoy of medical supplies to needy children in the heart of Africa. And the hundreds of volunteers who come to New Hampshire because they want to change the world may accomplish their goal as Capitol Hill policy advisors and political directors.

The bond of campaign camaraderie is formed without notice or fanfare. The compression of all aspects of your life into the sphere of the campaign world makes the network inescapable. Even when you're not "working" you find yourself sharing pizza with the volunteers, holidays with supporters, and drinks with the media, or swapping gossip with a rival campaign staffer. And as busy as it gets, nothing ever stands in the way of romance. When all you do is work, the only place you can fall in love is at work.

Your team members become too large a part of your life to simply be called co-workers. They are friends, and in most cases, friends for life. There is an unspoken understanding of the sanctity of these friendships. If a call for help goes out, it will never go unanswered.

WILL KANTERES

One thing I've been thinking about a lot lately is what this primary process does to friendships. A good friend is now with the Kerry campaign. In the 2002 New Hampshire election cycle we shared the duties of organizing the Manchester area. We were inseparable then, and now the different allegiances have divided us. We have become so ensconced in our own campaigns, our own offices, our own political environments, that regular phone calls and e-mails have nearly ceased. It is not for a lack of love or friendship; it's just one of those things, I guess. Last night we finally managed to have dinner together, and it was wonderful. We spent a couple hours catching up and talking in a totally partisan-free manner. It was so refreshing.

This morning I got to the office, and one of my campaign higher-ups was ready with a pad and pen to take down all the juicy details about the Kerry campaign that I might have gleaned from my dinner. "Who have they hired? Who's working where? Who's getting paid what?" and on and on. I found it really bothersome that a dinner between two close friends was seen as a reconnaissance mission. I guess for some there's no time to check allegiances at the door. We're putting so much into these campaigns, but being asked to act as a mole in my friendships outside the campaign is too much. For my own sanity, I hope I can keep relationships outside the Lieberman world alive.

—Christopher Pappas
NH Deputy Field Director, Lieberman campaign

The dynamics within the office are very interesting. My co-workers are all talented and hardworking, and I anticipate that the experience of working with them will be a good one. The unusual aspect is that, at least for the time being, I am the only woman in the office. Since I started here, I have been forced to learn how to throw a softball, catch a Frisbee, and duck when objects get thrown into the fans. At times it is like babysitting a group of eight-year-old boys. Most of the time they are well-behaved gentlemen, but there are those times when the eight-year-old boy overwhelms their system and causes them to hurl small objects into the fan just to see what will happen. It's an adventure, that's for sure!

—Kristina Saunders

I spend time with Dean at almost every event now. I guess I really knew that he knew me when we were leaving a house party and he put his hand on my shoulder and said, "You did a good job, Diesel." And I was like, "Oh my God, Governor Dean just called me Diesel." I didn't know how to react so I just said, "Thanks, Governor. Have a great trip. Good luck in Iowa."

I had another "Diesel" experience last week. The governor was in town, and he stopped by the office to do some call time. I walked in as he was finishing up. He stopped by my desk and said, "Diesel, I hear you're running Manchester Field now. That's great."

—Delana "Diesel" Jones
Manchester Regional Field Director, Dean campaign

[T]he seeds of political success are sown far in advance of any election day.... It is the sum total of the little things that happen which lead to eventual victory at the polls.
—J. Howard McGrath, Former Chairman,
Democratic National Committee, ca 1948

THE DOG DAYS OF SUMMER

BY MID-SUMMER, MANY OF THE CAMPAIGN STAFFERS FIND THEMSELVES FEELING A BIT LIKE THE PROVERBIAL TREE FALLING IN THE FOREST. THEY CAN'T HELP BUT WONDER:

If an organizer canvasses in the middle of the city, does anybody hear them? The campaigns are playing to a finite audience of about 2,010 people—the 2,000 New Hampshire activists who actually are aware of the upcoming Presidential election and about 10 reporters who are in New Hampshire sending back the prerequisite early field reports to their editors. These are times when you have to keep telling yourself that you are, indeed, working on a campaign for the Presidency of the United States. It's difficult to sense the aura of the Presidency when your candidate pays for something with a check and the cashier asks for identification, or when you find out that the only camera crew following your candidate that day is from the local high-school cable-access show. It doesn't help to turn to family and friends for support. You may call to tell them how amazing your candidate is and how he's going to win in a landslide even though the latest polls show him stuck in low single digits, only to have them talk about preparing your resume or the fast-approaching deadlines for applying to graduate schools.

It's natural to want to quantify how well each campaign is doing, so the staffers look for easy benchmarks.

Who can draw a crowd? Who beat whom in softball? Who had the best float or the catchiest chant at the July 4th parades? Which headquarters did George Stephanopoulos visit? Is it true that what's-his-name is going to endorse so-and-so? Why is the *Globe* only polling monthly? C-Span is coming to our event!

But you get through it because you know that, like the iceberg that sank the Titanic, 90 percent of your work on a campaign will remain just beneath the surface. You pick up the papers every day hoping to see a headline that cries out "X Surges in New Hampshire" from above the fold, but like the cry from the lookout on the deck of the Titanic, it rarely comes until the end of the voyage.

For Meryl and me, these are the halcyon days. Total access, no media cluster, and passionate, congenial participants. It is as if we discovered the world's finest surfing area—perfectly formed 6-foot swells, offshore breeze, 74-degree water, void of sharks, and only a handful of friendly fellow surfers on the beach. It won't last long. I've surfed this beach before and know all too well that four months from now, school lets out and the waters get so crowded, it's impossible to see the waves, let alone paddle out.

I'm sitting here in such a swirl—we've had the most amazing seven days. I can't believe that it was only last Monday when, at this very moment, we were heading to Burlington, Vermont for Dean's announcement. It seems like a million miles ago—this week has been surreal.

The energy of the announcement was HUGE and environmental, like an all-encompassing weather system. Not about any one individual, but something very large. Something is really clicking here.

—Karen Hicks
NH State Director, Dean campaign

After the announcement, we put together a two-day staff training. Given all that was going on, we were really concerned about pulling all of our field staff out of the field and sequestering them in a retreat. I'm really glad we didn't second-guess ourselves too much and we plowed ahead.

The first day, we revisited our original goals and then took a look at our progress to date. As remarkable as it is to have knocked on 20,000-plus doors, it comes nowhere near our goals. So, unless we have a transformation, we will fall far short of our plan to hit every Democratic and Independent door before the end of the summer.

We worked with Marshall Ganz, one of the most respected grassroots organizers in the country, on a day-long training. It was well worth it to pause and take stock of what is happening while we have the time and ability to redirect our resources. As a result, we're completely reengineering our field program, and all of the initiative came from our team. No getting dug in about not wanting to change our plan, or crazy harebrained ideas about how to do it— just smart people committed to figuring out how to get Howard Dean elected. It took us until late the second night to get there, but we did.

The first thing that is different about the program is that our staff will transition from being Howard Dean marketers to real organizers. They will develop relationships with supporters and help them act on their values in concert with other people. It starts by understanding people's personal stories— who are they, what are their life experiences, what are their values? Why are they interested in the campaign, and what do they potentially have to offer the campaign? Then we will ask our supporters to become opinion leaders in their social network by systematically reaching out to their entire social network through our house meeting program. They will reach out and say, "I'm on board with the Dean campaign. I'm organizing a meeting at my house, and I really want you to attend." So whether or not somebody attends, it's important voter contact because it signals, "Hey, my friend who I like or know is on board with Dean." This is more valuable than a stranger knocking on your door. It puts politics into people's living rooms and kitchens using language of everyday life. I know from previous work that the way you make a big number smaller is that you look at it over a time horizon and spread across many people. I think this has the potential to change the way people look at politics.

—Karen Hicks
NH State Director, Dean campaign

You meet the most interesting people canvassing door-to-door. It kind of makes me want to go home and start knocking on doors to see if it's just people in New Hampshire that are this interesting or if it's everywhere in America. There is hardly a day when someone doesn't come back with a funny or interesting story.

I ran into a woman one afternoon who asked if Gephardt was "the one with the red hair." I figured strawberry-blond qualified, so I said yes. "Yes, yes, I like him," she replied. I thought, that's a great way to know your candidate, not by his name, but by the color of his hair!

Then there was the man who kept taking more and more steps closer as I backed off his front porch, who somehow believed that "my candidate" was responsible for his "near-death experience."

And there was the winding lake road where I walked up onto the porch where a couple was sitting, and got so far as to say, "Hi, my name is Claire and I'm with the Dick Gephardt for President campaign," before I realized they were both sitting there stark naked. Ah, the joys of canvassing!

I think this is a job where you don't always see your individual results on a day-to-day basis. There aren't any gold stars going up by your name. It's definitely a team effort with gradual results. And the end result is Election Day. So maybe I did convert a Kerry or a Dean supporter, maybe I did make a Republican drop Bush by the wayside, maybe I did convince an undecided voter, but I think it was a combination of myself, and the intern who called them the next month, and the house party where the voter heard Dick speak. In the end, I have a part in working to elect the next Leader of the Free World, and that's just pretty darn cool.

—Claire Wilker
Volunteer/Intern Coordinator & Office Manager, Gephardt campaign

Recently, I was riding in the car with the senator. He was in a great mood, and he was getting more pumped up after each event we did. Maybe that was just a function of having 14 Diet Cokes in his body, but I don't think so. He kept saying, "I love this. This is what I'm all about. I love going to house parties. I love meeting people. I love getting out there and really talking to people. That's where I feel most comfortable, and that's where I feel I'm going to be the most successful. . ."

This sort of solidified it for me. This is what politics is all about. It sounds so silly and corny, but there is something to it. Here I am sitting next to a guy who could potentially be the next President of the United States and, hell, he's a senator and he's sitting in my parents' minivan which I've borrowed from them to drive him around the state. It's that sort of visceral fascination, having the opportunity to watch the whole thing transpire.

—Caleb Clark
NH Deputy State Director, Edwards campaign

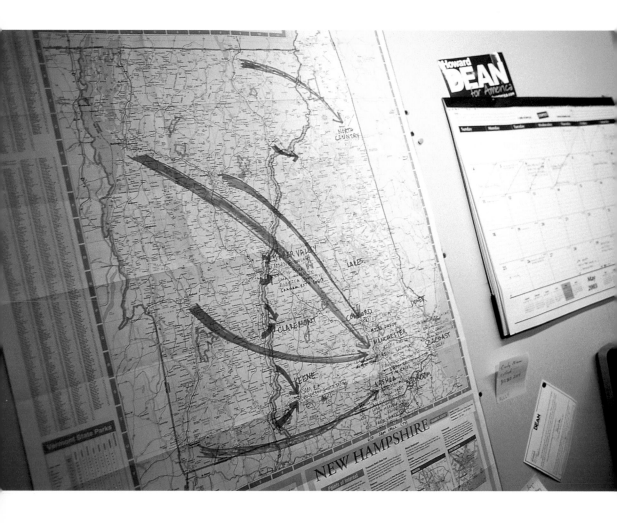

A couple of things this week sort of freaked me out. And it made me realize how much I'm acting like a firefighter. I'm struggling to put these trip days together for Dean, and I'm not thinking about content or strategy. I'm scrambling. I'm doing frontline work because I can't let go yet, partially because there just aren't enough of us.

I think it is hard to keep my eye on the original task of identifying 60,000 Howard Dean voters, while balancing all of these other demands which seem increasingly important. I'm not thinking enough about a three-month war plan at the end and how we are just going to be pummeled and how nasty the Kerry people are going to be towards us. I'm too busy figuring out what he's going to be doing next Tuesday.

Most of the staff is from outside New Hampshire. At this stage of the game, all of the campaigns are competing for about 3,000 of the hardcore activists. When we are generating call lists for Dean, I realize how many ridiculous details I know about the players here. Because of the primary, all of a sudden these details are valuable. If you're from out of state, then you probably don't know that it's hard to reach legislators on Tuesday, Wednesday, and Thursday, or that you shouldn't call Mary Louise Hancock [former state senator] too early in the morning, or that so-and-so's mother just died. These are things you can't train into people. At this early stage, given the intense competition for these potential supporters, the little details matter so much.

—Karen Hicks
NH State Director, Dean campaign

I couldn't wait for my first trip to New Hampshire. This is my third Presidential campaign, but my first primary. I had only visited the state for a couple of hours with Bill Clinton in the fall of 1992. This time I was staying for a few days and would get the full early-season experience.

For a political junkie, there is no place like New Hampshire. This is the state where Ed Muskie "cried" and got sent home. Here, Clinton said he would be with us until "the last dog died" (and he still is). Bill Bradley almost did a two-handed dunk on Al Gore, foretelling the difficulty my first paid political boss would have for the rest of that campaign. The place is filled with history.

The first day I was there in April, I stayed at the Center of New Hampshire Holiday Inn. I walked out of the elevator looking for Bob Graham and instead ran into a piece of that storied past. There, holding an interview in the lobby, was Gary Hart, who was then toying with the idea of running for President again. Seeing Hart in Manchester was like watching a surreal mix of past and present. I just smiled and thought to myself, "Welcome to New Hampshire."

—Jamal Simmons
Traveling Press Secretary, Graham campaign

Seventy-five million fans can't be wrong, right? NASCAR is the fastest growing sport in the country, and I've been told that three-quarters of all NASCAR fans admit to purchasing products that are advertised on the cars. So I guess it should seem like a natural fit for a Presidential candidate to advertise on the side of a NASCAR car (or truck, as the case may be). However, since it has never been done before, it seems to be drawing quite a bit of attention. Never before has a Presidential candidate so openly tried to capture the "NASCAR vote" and attract a whole new demographic of supporters. To that end, Bob Graham has plastered his campaign logo on the side of a Ford F-150 NASCAR Craftsman Series Truck and thereby made his campaign staffers instant NASCAR fans. Three weeks ago I couldn't even tell you what NASCAR stood for, much less anything about the sport. Now I can speak knowledgeably about the different types of races, the rules, and even the drivers. I still have a hard time agreeing with the idea that a car driving in a circle over and over and over again can be considered a sport, but I am beginning to understand the attraction. The speed, the noise, the excitement. What's not to love?

—Kristina Saunders
NH Deputy Press Secretary, Graham campaign

The New Hampshire primary is an extraordinary and exhilarating meeting of powerful politics with real voters. It ensures that no candidate or staffer is above dancing with a banner in a Main Street parade on a hot Fourth of July.

—Laura Memory Walters
NH Field Director, Edwards campaign

July 4th: Everybody loves a parade! Close to 100 people march with Governor Dean in the Amherst and Merrimack parades. We have the loudest, proudest float. The most signs. The most energy. And Dean is awesome. Senator Graham is a nice guy, and he says a genuine hello to everyone, including the crowd on the Dean truck. Lieberman is nice too, but he only says hello to non-political floats and folks. Kerry stays with his team for most of the time. But Dean, he's everywhere. Shaking hands. Waving at everyone. Giving impromptu speeches from the bullhorn. It was awesome (but the sunburn will last a week).

—Tom Hughes
NH Field Director, Dean campaign

T-minus two days until Congressman Gephardt's next trip to New Hampshire. For the last few weeks we have been preparing because it is longer and more elaborate than his past few trips up here. We are doing six house parties and going to the Nashua Pride baseball game. We will travel over 500 miles throughout New Hampshire. There is still a lot to do to make sure the train runs on time all weekend. Compared to some of the other Presidential campaigns here in New Hampshire, our staff is small, so everyone has to pitch in whenever the congressman is in town. All week we have event-logistics meetings at 8:30 pm where we go over the trip minute by minute.

The date is Sunday July 20. Congressman and Mrs. Gephardt and assorted staff and supporters are traveling in the RV. We are followed by a New Hampshire Public TV crew and freelance videographer. We have just finished a great house party in Derry and are on our way to the Nashua Pride baseball game. We have a few minutes to spare, and the congressman wants a sub sandwich, bad! In Londonderry, we find a small place called the Super Sub Shop. We pull this 30-foot RV right up to the front door and all of us disembark.

As we walk into this tiny shop, with this camera crew and entourage, I can see the lone employee's eyes just widen. This cute, young couple is sitting at a table having a quiet, late-afternoon lunch, and all of sudden they are surrounded by all of these people. Folks in New Hampshire are so lucky, and I'm not even sure they realize it. Where else in this enormous country can you be sitting in some out-of-the-way sandwich shop and get the unexpected opportunity to meet the man who could be the next President of the United States? And this happens up here every four years, and in season, it could happen almost every single day!

Back in the RV we know we still have 30 minutes until our scheduled arrival at the stadium, so we all take our time eating. This brief respite gives me a chance to really savor how lucky I am. I am 31 years old, and I am eating a sandwich and killing time with the man who, in my mind, will be the next President. The one thing that I try to tell all the interns and younger campaign staff is that candidates are very human, and they really are just like us. Because we see them on TV, and read about them in the national news magazines, it is so easy to think of these people as larger-than-life figures, when really they are very much like you and me . . . or maybe our parents!

As we pull up to Hollman Stadium in Nashua, we have tons of supporters and staff cheering and waving signs. I can see the congressman is also feeling the excitement. He loves baseball—I mean LOVES it. It's pretty clear that this chance to go to a game and throw out the first pitch is something he's been looking forward to all weekend. We have arranged for the congressman to wear a Nashua Pride jersey and hat and to announce batters over the stadium PA. It may not be the first pitch of the season, and it may not be major-league ball, but this is New Hampshire during Presidential primary season, and this is how modern Presidents are made. At least, we sure hope it is.

—Erik Greathouse
NH State Director, Gephardt campaign

Tensions can run high on a campaign. You're a family, there's no doubt about it—you spend every single day together for months, and you work at least 12 hours a day. Then after work you socialize with these same people. After all, you haven't had time to meet anyone outside of work. And finally, you end up heading home with some of the people because you're roommates as well.

And nothing makes tension higher than a big event, like the Nashua Pride game. It was supposed to be fun. Dick was scheduled to throw out the first pitch, and there would be food for our supporters. A pretty relaxing way to wrap up a busy weekend. And in the end we enjoyed ourselves a lot. Though the staff

was tired, we had to be "on" when all any of us wanted to do was grab something to eat, sit down, and watch the game—definitely not an option.

At that point, anything that's off just a little bit can be a high-stress situation—and it sure was that night. But I held it together: "Just grin and bear it." Everything worked out, and after a couple of innings of baseball we were all doing the YMCA together. I took note that our campaign is significantly better coordinated than our dance moves!

—Claire Wilker
Volunteer/Intern Coordinator & Office Manager, Gephardt campaign

This morning as I began to read the paper, I happened to glance at the masthead and date and realized that today is my brother's 33rd birthday. While I cringe that I remembered his birthday this way, I am just glad I remembered.

—Kristin Carvell
NH Press Secretary, Lieberman campaign

The whole State must be so well organized that every Whig can be brought to the polls. So divide the whole county into small districts and appoint in each, a committee. Make a perfect list of the voters and ascertain with certainty for whom they will vote. . . . Keep a constant watch on the doubtful voters and have them talked to by those in whom they have the most confidence. . . . On election days see that every Whig is brought to the polls.
—Abraham Lincoln, 1840

In addition to the badge of honor campaign staffers earn ·from their service here, they leave with a post-graduate-level skill set that they can, and will, apply to all of their future endeavors. They learn by instruction— from their campaign managers and co-workers, and by experience—from the day-to-day, hands-on work during the process. They must be prepared to deal with almost any crisis. Try standing in front of 350 hungry Democrats at a $100-a-plate county committee dinner and explaining why your candidate's vote on an ethanol bill in the Senate is more important than honoring them at their annual fundraiser. Or, try maintaining your campaign's plotted course and message, while dealing with daily attacks from the press, the opposition, and in some cases, your own staff. Would you like to run a $2.4 million organization with only one source of revenue—the benevolence of your supporters? These marketing, manage-ment, and finance lessons form a grueling course load for one semester. And that's just the Science of Politics. The Art of Understanding Human Nature is taught 24/7 on the campaign trail. The training is tough, but it keeps you sharp.

The average age in this year's corps is about 24, and with good reason. Physically and mentally, a 24-year-old

politico can function on four hours of sleep, a steady intake of Diet Coke and Dunkin' Donuts all day, and multiple pints of discounted draft beer at the pub at night. Granted, just as John McEnroe still has the talent necessary to compete on center court, there are always "elder statesmen" willing to put in long hours on the campaigns. But the ones who I know often sleep at their own homes or in comfortable hotel rooms. Most will admit they'd still be typing their memos on IBM Selectrics and calling in from the road on rotary-dial pay phones if it weren't for the technical guidance of their 19-year-old assistants. The choice is clear: absorb the new technology or face the prospect of becoming simply a name on a 3x5 card, or a nanobyte in a database—a fate that is even more depressing than it sounds. Stay in the game too long, and you run the risk of feeling like an aging McEnroe sweating alcohol under the noon sun while a 15-year-old, who can't even legally drive his new Hummer, fires 127-mph serves at you from across the net on center court.

The young operatives depart fully trained and battle tested. They are the human resource so vital to the national parties—the commandos who will go out and manage races for future governors, senators, or, if they persevere, Presidents.

There was a two-week period when people were literally lined up outside of my office. All I did was answer question after question after question. It felt like I'd given birth to 35 young adults. We have to figure out a way to help them think things through at a more fundamental level and come up with their own answers—within reason, of course.

We've been taking staffers out for coffee or a meal and going over the values we've adopted as a campaign. We ask people to reflect on how they are doing in each of those areas, where are they really strong, where they think they need to do a little better, and how we can best support them. It's amazing how smart everybody is, for the most part, and how much we learn during these meetings. I think there is recognition that if we are going to win, we have to do things a little bit differently. It's starting to take shape, and it's so exciting to see.

—Karen Hicks
NH State Director, Dean campaign

When you are in charge of the field operation, your work is all about when the candidate is not around. It is during these times that you have volunteer activities, make phone calls to crowd-build for events, and expand your organizational structure.

Trip days are like an Election Day—where you see all of your plans, the calls you have made, the crowds you have built—come to fruition. The execution of your plans is like riding down a water slide—the momentum naturally carries you along. I start to feel happy and relaxed on the night before a trip because most of the things that are my responsibility are then beyond my control. My struggle is that the day after a trip, I inevitably wake up far too early because my mind is racing with thoughts about how we are going to handle the next one.

—Laura Memory Walters
NH Field Director, Edwards campaign

So many active New Hampshire Democrats can trace their original political involvement back to a Presidential primary, to some Presidential candidate who somehow sparked their political interest and got them involved. Whether it was John F. Kennedy, Gene McCarthy, or any other of the host of people who've run over the years. The huge plus to us here is that it brings in new blood every four years. People get inspired and want to get involved.

—Ray Buckley
Eastern Regional Political Director, Lieberman campaign

Thank God it isn't raining. It's really hot and humid though. And windy. Still could rain. Boy, I hope it doesn't rain. It's a little tense before the big event.

I was trying to get some tape for the curtains to make sure they didn't blow open. I should have realized we'd have 80 people standing on the risers and the curtains wouldn't even show. But by that point, the key parts of the event were out of my hands.

You hope the plane lands on time, but can't control it. You hope there's not traffic on the drive from the airport, but can't control it. You hope a thousand Teamster union members come pumped up and ready to help Dick win, but can't control it. You hope Hoffa and Dick make the rally speeches of their lives, but can't control it. Turns out the plane was on time, there was no traffic, a thousand Teamsters showed up ready to rock, and Dick gave the kind of knock-'em-dead speech that makes people say, "That's Dick Gephardt?" I love it when he does that.

—Kathy Roeder
NH Communications Director, Gephardt campaign

lding a Better Future for
all Working Men and
Women

SECRETARY / TREASURER
PRINCIPAL OFFICER
NEW ENGLAND

D W. LAUGHTON
TERS JOINT COUNCIL 10

Kerry
CORPS
Volunteer
OF THE
WEEK
JUNE
JULY
AUGUST
SEPTEMBER
OCTOBER
John Kerry
PRESIDENT
www.johnkerry.com
John Kerry
PRESIDENT
HEY!
GRAB
AND
THE

I've been having a tough time on the campaign the last few weeks. As our campaign team grows, and we bring on people that are older and more experienced then me, I feel like I have a target on my back. I am one of the youngest people on the campaign but have a position that is very high up in the campaign hierarchy. I'm very lucky to have the position I do, but because I am so young I'm feeling a lot of resentment.

I've concluded that there are two types of campaigning that take place on a campaign. One, of course, is for the candidate. The other is internal and more under the radar, but equally important and usually more vicious. I'm talking about individual campaigns by staffers for power and status within the organization. In a way I guess it makes sense because in general it takes certain types of people to work on campaigns—aggressive, driven, competitive, and willing to let their jobs be their lives. So it's only natural that these qualities would come out in people within a campaign and in dealings with co-staffers. Also, in this business your next job—particularly if you want to stay in the campaign side of politics—almost always comes from people you've worked with or for, not necessarily through your candidate's winning. So there is just as much incentive to campaign internally as there is for your candidate.

I know that I do both types of campaigning—you have to if you want to be successful. But it gets tiring, especially during a Presidential campaign in New Hampshire when you're spending all your time—work and leisure—with campaign people and you are usually friends with the people you must compete against, both on other campaigns and within your own.

—Emily Silver
NH Deputy State Director & Chief of Staff, Lieberman campaign

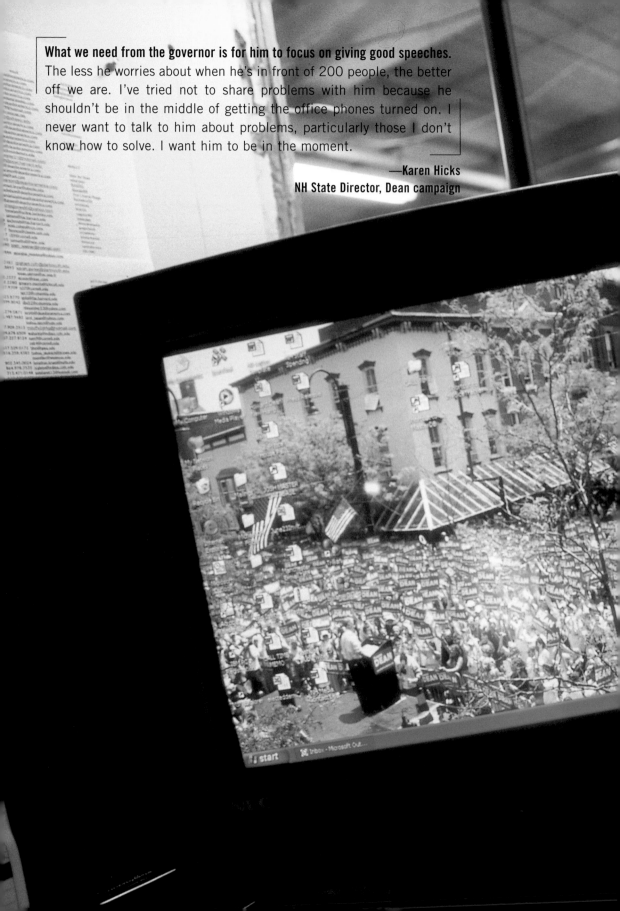

What we need from the governor is for him to focus on giving good speeches. The less he worries about when he's in front of 200 people, the better off we are. I've tried not to share problems with him because he shouldn't be in the middle of getting the office phones turned on. I never want to talk to him about problems, particularly those I don't know how to solve. I want him to be in the moment.

—Karen Hicks
NH State Director, Dean campaign

Sometimes I still wonder if I'm crazy to postpone my senior year of college to work on a Presidential campaign. I gave up plans to move into an apartment with my best friends at college. I won't walk down the avenue at graduation with the people who became my family away from home. Going back to finish up will never be the same. I know that working on this campaign is a once-in-a-lifetime opportunity, but there are still moments when I think about the once-in-a-lifetime experiences I am losing out on. It's times like these when it really hits home that not all choices in life are easy.

I got an e-mail the other day from one of my college friends talking about getting ready to go back for senior year. I hadn't even realized that the summer was almost over! At night, when I lie in bed, before I fall asleep, I think of what my friends are doing back home during this last full summer break of their lives. I begin to wonder what I will miss out on as I continue to work on this campaign. And then I wake up, go to work, and I get caught up in the thrill of the campaign again. I'm beginning to think that for a roller coaster of emotions, there is no better place to work than on a campaign.

—Claire Wilker
Volunteer/Intern Coordinator & Office Manager, Gephardt campaign

In the middle of the afternoon on July 10, I answered my phone and heard Governor Dean's voice on the other end of the line. He had called to ask if I had chosen to stay on the campaign after the summer until the primary. I said yes. It was the first time I had said it out loud to anyone. Up until then I had toyed with the idea of taking time off to continue working, but when others asked me about my decision, I usually said, "I'm still thinking about it." I'd roll my eyes at the thought of dealing with my supportive but concerned family, explaining my nontraditional semester to my friends, and pleading with Hamilton College to allow me to stay on the campaign and graduate with my classmates.

On the back wall of the office, tucked in an unseen corner, is a timeline featuring the most important pictures and dates of our campaign. On May 19, a small Polaroid picture of my face became part of that colorful, handmade poster. Since then, many pictures and milestones have been added, and I can't imagine not continuing to participate in the story of this campaign. Watching from my college dorm room would never have been an option.

—Rachel Sobelson
Office Manager, Dean campaign

In my few years working on campaigns I've heard one line over and over: "The most important things in any political race are people, money, and time." And I've learned that everything you want or need to do stems from these three. You can always find more people and money—you can't find more time. Time—months, days, hours, minutes—and how you utilize it until the voting booths close on Election Day is the most critical aspect of any race. In the life of an individual staffer, that means that time spent not working is potentially hurting the candidate and the campaign. There is always more to do, and there is pressure on all of us.

Yet this obsession with time makes you realize that time is passing not just inside the campaign world but outside in the "real world" as well. By spending all my days trying to help elect my candidate President of the United States, I've already missed out on some pretty important things in my non-campaign life—supporting a friend at his grandmother's funeral, attending my nephew's eighth birthday party, and spending time with my parents.

I feel guilty whatever I choose to do, because I know that I won't be able to get back the time I'm missing in either world. I try to maintain a balance, knowing that campaigns are always short-term. In the bubble of Manchester, New Hampshire, surrounded by others who care so deeply about and understand the importance of this Presidential race, it's easy to forget that time has not stopped in the real world. Losing myself in the campaign is a sacrifice I've made in order to be in this business and to be part of the democratic process. I just hope that I can find my way home when all this is over.

—Emily Silver
NH Deputy State Director & Chief of Staff, Lieberman campaign

It's one o'clock in the morning. I'm exhausted. But I can't sleep. My days are so consumed with this campaign and Dick Gephardt that I never get a chance to stop and think. The minute I turn off the lights and crawl into bed, my brain kicks into high gear. I lay in bed wondering what my nonpolitical friends and family members are up to. I wonder when I'll get a chance to see them again and hope that it'll be soon. But, then my thoughts turn back to the campaign. Questions fill my head as I fight them and try to sleep. Am I doing enough? What can I do better? Is our campaign doing enough? Was my event today good

enough? The thoughts roll from one to another for what seems like hours, until it's impossible to have another thought and I finally drift off to sleep. It's not a deep sleep, but it's sleep nonetheless.

Tomorrow I'll wake up and won't remember what I was worrying about. I'll go through my day, work my ass off, and then try again for sleep. I'll be optimistic that this is the night I'll get the sleep I've been looking for. But there's always something else that will keep me awake half the night—proof of the fact that campaign life truly is a 24-hour-a-day job.

—Katie Kiernan
Southern NH Regional Field Director, Gephardt campaign

This week I parallel parked for the first time, exactly five months after I had my first cup of coffee, which was also my first official day of work at headquarters on McGregor Street. This whole campaign has been about "firsts." Every day, I need to take on a task that I've never tried before. But there is a part of me that believes that this campaign experience is more like college than anyone wants to admit.

—Rachel Sobelson
Office Manager, Dean campaign

The idea that you can merchandise candidates for high office like breakfast cereal—that you can gather votes like box tops—is, I think, the ultimate indignity to the democratic process.

—Adlai E. Stevenson

IT'S MY HOUSE PARTY AND I'LL CRY IF I WANT TO

FOR DECADES, NEW HAMPSHIRE VOTERS HAVE GATHERED IN THE HOMES OF THEIR NEIGHBORS TO MEET AND EVALUATE THE PRESIDENTIAL CANDIDATES SEEKING THEIR PARTY'S NOMINATION.

"House parties" traditionally provide an intimate setting for groups of 10 to 50 people to meet and assess a candidate. At the same time, they give the campaign staff direct access to high concentrations of party activists and community opinion leaders from which to draw upon and strengthen their local campaign.

To the untrained eye, these receptions appear the same: red, white, and blue balloons; sign-in sheets; bumper stickers; buttons; policy "white papers"; chocolate-chip cookies; and rubbery, dice-size cubes of white, yellow, and speckled cheeses. The host welcomes and introduces the candidate, alluding to his achievements and stature, but subtly reminding him and the guests that, for the next 45 minutes, he is just one of them. The candidate speaks, holds a Q & A session and, hopefully, the audience applauds politely.

It's that simple, at first glance. You have to look deeper to see if the candidate is making any real progress in his effort to win voters. Do people search out the staff to volunteer time and support, or does the staff have to grab people and ask for their commitment as they try to slip out the side door? Do people run home as soon as they hear, "Thank you very much and I really want your vote on January 27"? And if they do linger after the candidate leaves, are they talking about the candidate or just catching up with their neighbors? (If you overhear the words Red Sox, Patriots, foliage, or Home Depot, it's the latter.)

Most campaigns arrange for four or five of these homogeneous parties each time the candidate is in the state. They can be tedious for campaign staffers (how many times a week can you listen to your candidate's stump speech?), and unspectacular, as they're rarely intended to attract national press attention. The last thing a press secretary wants to hear at one of these events is the question, "Did he really mean to say what he just said?" posed by a *New York Times* reporter. Inevitably, it happens. Candidates do get tired and have been known to let their guard down for a brief moment in these relaxed settings. Attend enough of these parties and you're bound to see a candidate offend or snap at a questioner, misstate his personal achievements, or surprise his policy wonks by announcing a new tax plan or foreign-policy initiative.

Staffers react like a political SWAT team, scurrying around during the next couple of days, trying to explain to supporters and countless media outlets that what the candidate meant to say was . . .

More important, these mini dramas offer the astute voter a glimpse of the candidate's personality and thought process in its purest form, without the imprint of speechwriters, media coaches, or image consultants. The candidate's statement may confirm a voter's existing doubts about character or policies or may raise new concerns. The manner in which the candidate and staff handle the incidents often determines how voters respond. These subtleties are precisely what observers must look for if they hope to accurately read the tea leaves at a New Hampshire house party.

Perhaps the surest sign that your candidate's support will multiply over the coming months is the sight of real people crying real tears—a sight that seemed more pervasive during the 2004 campaign than in past primaries. Understanding why these folks are crying helps to explain the inspiration, passion, and commitment of New Hampshire voters and activists. I believe these tears are not simply the result of the public's fear and frustration during these uncertain times. It's said that if you go to the opera and don't cry, then you don't get opera. The same is true of politics.

Each campaign is a story. It may be reported as a message, a cause, or a movement, but voters sense the tale viscerally and it either resonates with their lives or falls flat. It is human nature to look for a reflection of our own lives in our popular parables. It's what worked for mythology and what works for Hollywood. Voters want their leader and the essence of the campaign to mirror their values, hopes, dreams—essentially their lives. The candidates are the main characters, but they share the stage with the staff and supporters that surround them. So in the end, the New Hampshire house party provides an off-off-off Broadway stage for the campaign to tell its story. Live theater at its best, and if the audience buys the story, if the joy and sorrow of the campaign are well received in tryouts, the campaign gets to take the show on the road.

WILL KANTERES

Congressman Gephardt was in town this past weekend. Getting to see him in action, speaking to people at house parties, was amazing. To hear him talk passionately about what he believes in gives me renewed energy to go out and work and make sure he becomes our next President. I feel like he could be the next FDR, and to be able to see that, and in some small way be a part of making that happen, is one of the coolest feelings. It seems to me that he is the kind of man children grow up dreaming about and wishing to have as their President. I guess all campaign staffers feel that way about their candidates, but maybe only crazy politicos like me ever dreamed as a child of what they wished their President were like.

—Claire Wilker
Volunteer/Intern Coordinator & Office Manager, Gephardt campaign

Staffing the senator at events like this is great. You hear what he is saying to everyone, how he works the room. It's about as retail as it gets. It is tiring though, even for me; I imagine it must be very hard on him sometimes. People are amazed at how personable and charming he is one on one. He's a pretty cool guy—alpha male all the way—and it's hard not to like him.

Moving him through the crowd can be tough. He wants to answer everyone's questions, but he also wants to meet everyone in the room, and it's difficult to do that in two hours, let alone one. Lots of people will ask him three or four questions in a row when they meet him. They think this is their big chance, that they will never see him again, so better ask now!

—**Theo Yedinsky**
NH Political Director, Kerry campaign

So much of this is not about the work. The work itself—making phone calls, going door-to-door, putting up yard signs—is not brain surgery. What is hard is keeping everyone motivated and energized since so much work must be done in an awfully short period of time. For this reason, being a field director can feel a lot like being a parent. You need to make sure you give the staff the opportunity to offer enough input so they feel ownership, but not so much that they get completely off track. Let them make their own mistakes, but not on anything too important. Make sure they are reasonably happy and satisfied, but do not baby them because the job is tough and that won't change. Figure out who really needs a day off and who is being lazy. You need to know when to

address a bad call in public and when to let it go or talk about it later. When to utilize staff input and when to cast it aside because you do know best, which is why you are the boss. When to confirm and verify that staffers have done something and when you can just trust that they have.

A highly focused and energized field staff is even more important on a small campaign like ours. We need everyone to be able to do a bit of everything and have precious little room for error. Our campaign is fortunate—every single one of our field staffers is fantastic. If you hire strong people, that is more than half the battle. Luckily, we did just that.

—Laura Memory Walters
NH Field Director, Edwards campaign

There are days to canvass, and then there are days not to canvass. Days when the sun is shining, when it's not too hot or too cold and New Hampshire is ablaze in color. And then days when it's raining and cold and dark at 2 pm. There are days when people are out mowing their grass, and they smile as you come up to talk to them. And days when they open their doors and stare at you, cold and wet, like you're crazy. We canvass regardless of the weather, because that's how we win this thing, door by door, voter by voter.

It seems the weekends are mostly the wet, cold kinds. We canvass alone—you can hit more doors that way. And so I'm standing alone on a Sunday afternoon in the pouring rain, holding my umbrella in the crook of my arm as I try to mark down the result of my last conversation. Utter darkness creeps up on me—after all, it's 4:15 in November. My walk lists are curling at the edges because it's damp, and the ink is smearing on the pages because my umbrella has a broken spoke and so rain is pouring down on my shoulder.

This can be a lonely job. A loneliness that hits home even more as I knock on door after door and see people who peer out at me from an upstairs window but refuse to answer the door; homes where lamps are lit and the smell of Sunday dinner creeps out as they tell me they don't have time to talk but take my literature and then quickly shut the door. Leaving me outside, alone, in the rain, with my broken umbrella . . . and it's getting colder.

And there are the little old ladies who ask me why I am out in this weather, tell me to go home—aren't you cold, you should get a heavier coat, it's getting late. . . . They're sweet. They're trying to be helpful, but in the end I still have my walk packet to finish and I'm not going home until it's done, even though it's cold, it's wet, it's getting dark.

But I finish. I come back to the office, trickle in with the others, who like me, are wet and cold. "It's pretty gross out there." "It's terrible." "I don't understand why it always rains on weekends." We make some event turnout calls for tomorrow's trip with Dick as we dry out and then head out to Margarita's to don sombreros and sing "Happy Birthday" to Anna, laughing, joking, and this is anything but a lonely job.

—Claire Wilker
Volunteer/Intern Coordinator & Office Manager, Gephardt campaign

I spent a few days this week packing up my summer clothes and other items that I brought with me to New Hampshire but realize now I'll never need or use. I'm giving some things to my family who are here visiting to take home with them and mailing some others to friends to hang onto for me. I want to pare everything down so that on January 28 I can go to the next primary state with just my stereo and a few suitcases in my car.

At an event today a voter asked me where I live. "Manchester for 100 more days," I answered. After January 27, I guess the most permanent address I'll have is my e-mail—or maybe my license plate number!

—Kathy Roeder
NH Communications Director, Gephardt campaign

The very public secret of the Graham campaign at this point in the evolving history of the contest for the 2004 Democratic Presidential nomination is that we have money troubles. The very private secret of the Graham campaign at this point is that things are worse than that.

Faith is a hell of a thing. It endlessly demands investment of a man's most precious things—his soul and his time. Its payoff—almost absurdly—lies not in what it has promised but in its promise. What most people don't understand about Bob Graham is that he is truly faithful. And it is his faith which largely inspires my own substantial faith in this campaign.

Graham launched his candidacy preaching of the deception, power abuse, and corruption in the Bush White House. I am here in New Hampshire as an early acolyte of his gospel. As I now read daily of White House scandals as well as the supposedly imminent peril of the Graham political enterprise, I find myself reduced to a singular response: "A-men."

—Chris Smith
Manchester Field Director, Graham campaign

Driving up to the office this morning, it struck me again, as it has so often recently, how odd it is that I am parking in the same spot, showing up to the same office, answering the same phone and yet doing it all for a different candidate. When Bob Graham dropped out of the race, I thought briefly about closing the book on my New Hampshire primary experience. However, I soon realized that an escape from the cold New Hampshire winter was not in my future. Many of the former Graham staffers quickly moved over to the Clark campaign, and all the pieces seemed to fall into place for me to join them. I had gotten involved in this process intending to see it out to the primary, and if my first candidate dropped out, it made sense to look for a new one. The goal remained the same—remove George Bush from office—though the vehicle for doing that had changed.

The differences between the Graham campaign and the Clark campaign are noticeably drastic. As soon as the Clark campaign got going, supporters and volunteers started pouring through the doors. There is an energy and excitement that is palpable. It feels like a real campaign. It feels possible.

—Kristina Saunders
NH Deputy Communications Director, Clark campaign

After the Graham campaign ended, I joined the Clark team. My first trip back to New Hampshire after that was intense. I was still learning my new candidate, his issues, and his rhythms. Remarkably, the initial uncertainty gave way when I saw Steve Bouchard and Kristina Saunders, both refugees from the Graham campaign who were now with Camp Clark. I knew General Clark and I would be in good hands.

I am ready for the energy and excitement of New Hampshire again, and Wes Clark is providing both.

—Jamal Simmons
Traveling Press Secretary, Clark campaign

Gephardt for President . . . Gephardt for President . . . This is Claire . . . I work for Gephardt . . . Hi, my name is Claire and I am calling with the Gephardt for President Campaign . . . Hi, I'm with Gephardt for President and I wanted to stop by today to . . . Gephardt for President . . . I'm with Gephardt . . . Gephardt . . . Gephardt . . . Breathe Gephardt, dream Gephardt, live Gephardt.

And so I sing. Alone in the car as I am driving out to canvass or to run campaign errands. With the radio turned all the way up as loud as I can bear, country, rap, pop, it doesn't matter as long as the station is playing a song that I know most of the words to. I sing, even though I can't carry a tune. I hear myself torture a song as I try to hit a high note there was no way I could ever make. And I laugh, a real laugh, not the slight chuckle that I so often hear coming from my lips now, but a deep, carefree laugh, the kind that used to burst out every day for one reason or another. And sometimes as I walk down the street to work, or on my way to canvass, I sing. I sing to laugh from inside myself again. I sing to remind myself that I still am, in the end, Claire. Nothing more, nothing less. The Gephardt campaign is a part of me, a deep and integral one, but it does not completely define who I am. Hi, my name is Claire.

—Claire Wilker
Volunteer/Intern Coordinator & Office Manager, Gephardt campaign

One of the things that has been difficult lately is responding to the questions I get from family, friends, and regional field staffers who ask about the state of our campaign. Of course, we're far from the top of the pack in New Hampshire, and I get many questions from people who think we're dropping out or on the brink of doing so. I feel like many times I go right into spin mode and talk about how we lead in most national polls, how we're doing well in other states, etc. What is frustrating is having to refute their arguments or observations when I feel and/or fear some of the same things. What has been reassuring lately, though, is how fluid this race remains. I think 75 percent of the state is either uncommitted or soft in their support. This thing could turn on its head five times before January 27.

The race is almost like that old New England adage: "If you don't like the weather, just wait a few minutes and it will change." For now, I'm glad to wait a few minutes and see what the next pattern will hold for our campaign.

—Christopher Pappas
NH Deputy Field Director, Lieberman campaign

Polling: the crack of the campaign world. You try to pretend you don't need it, don't care about it, especially when it's bad. But when it's good, your entire perspective on life changes and you can't try to pretend it doesn't.

In general, we stay grounded about how we measure success and movement. Polls really are just snapshots of different universes of people. Our definition of our movement is in hard numbers: numbers of phone calls to voters, numbers of new people who turn out to events, numbers of new supporters, numbers of meetings held with supporters. As long as those numbers keep moving up, so does our optimism.

—Kristyn McLeod
NH Political Director, Edwards campaign

What I'm doing now surprises me—not that I am following politics, but that I'm working in it. I argued for Mondale in fourth grade. I played Dukakis in our junior-high mock Presidential debate. In high school and college I volunteered on campaigns: I phone banked, I canvassed, I assembled lawn signs, I went to rallies and meetings. Despite all these obvious signs that I was a prime candidate for working in politics, nobody ever said to me, "Hey, did you know that one day you could get paid for this?" And I never asked. I spent a teeny amount of time on mock trial at school, and all my teachers said, "You should be a lawyer." That sounded right to me.

Jobs in politics don't run in the classifieds, and they aren't promoted by high school or college career centers. No one ever tells you the chain of command

in a political operation, how you can work up the ladder, the different kinds of jobs available in media, fundraising, field work, or public policy. The good news is that political jobs are not impossible to find or get. In fact I think getting a job in politics is surprisingly democratic. You don't have to have a legacy last name or a parent in the Senate to get an an entry-level job. Candidates and political parties always need energetic, passionate young people who will work for terrible salaries under bizarre conditions.

Young people need to know that if they're the kind of people who are always ranting about injustice, the Bill of Rights, democratic values, and how things "ought to be," they do have options.

—Kathy Roeder
NH Communications Director, Gephardt campaign

This may sound weird, but with only 64 days to go, all this anticipation feels a little like we're waiting for someone to have a baby. You know something big is about to happen, but you don't know how it's going to turn out or exactly what impact it will have on your life. There are hundreds of campaign staffers in New Hampshire, and all of them believe (or should anyway) that it will be their final phone call, knock on a door, visibility, autocall, mail piece, or scheduling decision that will put their candidate over the top.

—Kristyn McLeod
NH Political Director, Edwards campaign

Having been through the New Hampshire primary before when I worked for Al Gore in 2000, I know all too well what is about to come. I can't help but think about what life will be like after January 27. Having won the New Hampshire primary in 2000 after an extraordinarily close battle with Bill Bradley, and having lost the general election so bitterly, I know what both success and defeat are like.

Even if we do well, things will change. The campaign becomes bigger. It becomes national. You no longer have the control and the influence we have at this stage. It becomes more media focused and less voter focused. You have to specifically construct photo ops instead of specifically constructing settings where the candidate can answer questions from as many voters as possible. Gone will be the days where you carefully coordinate a one-on-one meeting with

a former local school-board member. Gone will be the days where you ask around to borrow a car to pick up the candidate from the airport later that afternoon. The Secret Service will descend, national media will follow even more closely, bigwigs will become even bigger and more important. Everything will be taken up a notch. There will be more people between the voters and the candidate. More people between you and the candidate, no matter who you are, no matter how high you have risen in the ranks.

The primaries after New Hampshire and Iowa, and even the battleground states in the general election, are simply not as labor intensive. They are media states where grassroots organizing and Get Out the Vote (GOTV) efforts are not as effective, so there is less that staff can do to make a difference.

And if you lose the election, well, I know how bad that sucks, too.

—Laura Memory Walters
NH Field Director, Edwards campaign

Where is everyone? I'm in the community room at Arel Manor in Nashua just before a town hall meeting with Congressman Gephardt. The room has been set up. The chairs are in a perfect semicircle with a path down the middle; the banner is in the front of the room perfectly centered, and the room has the proper signage. So, I wait and feel an anxiety attack come on. Where the hell is everyone who told me they were coming? It's OK, I tell myself, because Dick will be late, as always, and people will filter in. It's going to be OK.

My phone rings. They're almost here. People continue to come in, but I'm not happy. I want it packed. I want people to leave thinking, wow, where did all those people come from? Slowly, the room fills and it's OK. It always is. Dick walks in, shakes hands, and walks to the front of the room. My panic slowly subsides. It always does when Dick starts to speak.

I feel like I've heard Dick Gephardt speak a thousand times. During his speech, I always know the next words out of his mouth. I can tell when they've tweaked his speech or changed words to make it sound more powerful. I hear Dick speak when he's in New Hampshire, and I watch him on TV when he's not here. There are no surprises for me. But, still, I get chills when I hear him, because I've never agreed with anyone more on the issues, because I hear the passion in his voice that resonates throughout the room.

I look around and see people nodding and clapping. The room may not be as full as I'd like, but these people get it. And I get chills because I am so proud that I work for this man.

—Katie Kiernan
Southern NH Regional Field Director, Gephardt campaign

Less than two months left. We've built a great operation. 12 offices. More than 100 staff. 930 house meetings conducted to date. More than 5,200 one-on-one meetings. Tens of thousands of supporters identified in the database. Every day more people join the organization. If we're lucky enough to keep going like we have been, we'll win.

But we aren't going to win this on luck, and 59 days is an eternity in New Hampshire primary politics. There is an enormous amount of work to do. Most people are just beginning to pay attention. And I'm certain that the other

campaigns will start blasting Howard Dean with everything in their opposition research books right about . . . NOW!

Most of my time is spent in the office now. It's exciting to see this group of people who, for the most part, had tremendous passion and energy but precious little experience grow into an unparalleled team. But it's a little sad for me that we are almost at the end, and I may never have the opportunity to shape something like this again.

—Tom Hughes
NH Field Director, Dean campaign

For the past five weeks, I have been an employee of Clark For President, Inc. This, of course, is after having been employed by Graham For President, Inc., a week prior to Clark.

Same election. Same office space. And many of the same people. Different candidate. Different responsibilities. A different spirit and a new hope.

In the popular imagination, people like me—that is, people who work on political campaigns professionally—are believed to be whores of a sort. Given the right price, we'll turn a trick and perform our service for anyone. In contrast, the common fantasy among people like me is that we all are in this for reasons so righteous and noble as to be unrooted from the sodden earth.

The truth is that at some early point, my naked need for money was greater than my pure belief in General Clark. The truth also is that my love of justice and my lust for victory shall always exceed both. And now, at this late point, my belief in General Clark is also very great.

The rhythms of life on the campaign trail are so instinctive, so basic and primal, that when travelers—that select group—fall off horses, they find it relatively easy to remount and pick up the forward beat.

—Chris Smith
State Canvass Director, Clark campaign

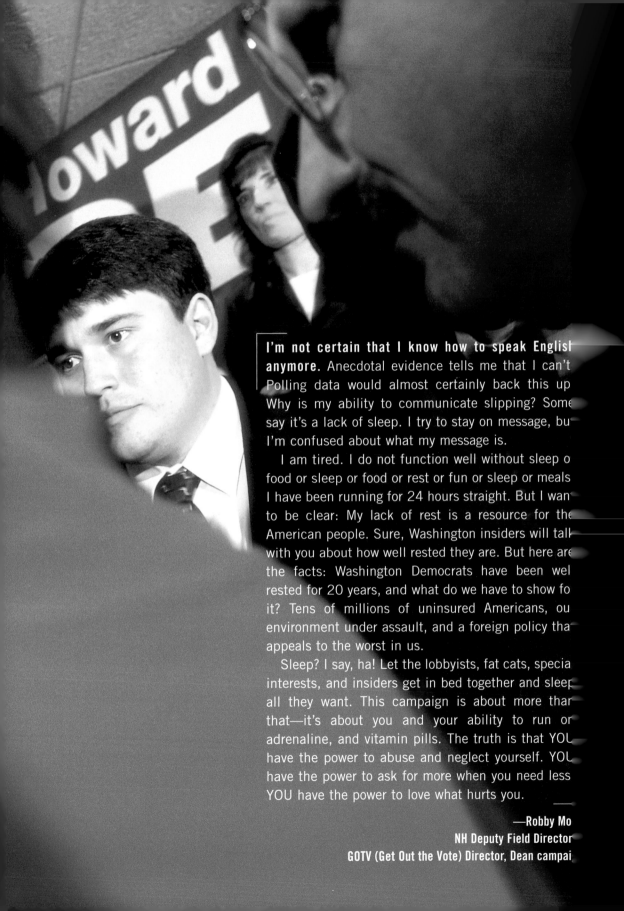

I'm not certain that I know how to speak English anymore. Anecdotal evidence tells me that I can't. Polling data would almost certainly back this up. Why is my ability to communicate slipping? Some say it's a lack of sleep. I try to stay on message, but I'm confused about what my message is.

I am tired. I do not function well without sleep or food or sleep or food or rest or fun or sleep or meals. I have been running for 24 hours straight. But I want to be clear: My lack of rest is a resource for the American people. Sure, Washington insiders will talk with you about how well rested they are. But here are the facts: Washington Democrats have been well rested for 20 years, and what do we have to show for it? Tens of millions of uninsured Americans, our environment under assault, and a foreign policy that appeals to the worst in us.

Sleep? I say, ha! Let the lobbyists, fat cats, special interests, and insiders get in bed together and sleep all they want. This campaign is about more than that—it's about you and your ability to run on adrenaline, and vitamin pills. The truth is that YOU have the power to abuse and neglect yourself. YOU have the power to ask for more when you need less. YOU have the power to love what hurts you.

—Robby Mo
NH Deputy Field Director
GOTV (Get Out the Vote) Director, Dean campai

There were a few days back there that I was all for quitting. Forget how much I admire Dick Gephardt. Forget how much I want him to get this nomination and defeat George Bush in 2004. Someone else could do it. Someone else could work every day, someone else could give up her family and friends, someone else could be so exhausted and frustrated some days she just didn't want to go on. And then there was the voice inside me that said, "I am not a quitter." Then there were the voices of my friends that said, "You don't have to do this. You can come home any time. You have other things you can do, like finish school."

But I am not a quitter. Still, this is hard. This is damn hard. And while I knew ahead of time what I was getting into, I honestly had no idea until I was in it what it could really be like. What kicks you in the butt, what makes you get over it, is knowing other staffers are feeling the same things. And not just people on your own staff but people on other campaigns. Because candidate rivalry or not, we're all in the same boat; we're all going through much of the same thing. That helps—it helps a lot. And a couple of weeks later, I'm back on top again.

—Claire Wilker
Volunteer/Intern Coordinator & Office Manager, Gephardt campaign

It's 2 am, the night of the first New Hampshire snowstorm, and I'm shoveling snow from the driveway at the house where I'm staying. I am lucky to have a bed to sleep in at the home of one of our supporters—many staff members have had to settle for floors. The least I can do is help out and shovel, even if so much snow is falling that no one may notice my efforts when the household wakes up in the morning.

This is not a glamorous job. The Edwards team is lean and hardworking, but New Hampshire residents are used to the political season and they have let us know that they are not ready to pay close attention. Our staff must promote events that may get little to no coverage. No, not glamorous at all. Yet we plug away and uncover more reasons for the average citizen to meet Senator Edwards, who may well be the next President of the United States. And I shovel the snow because being late for work is not an option.

—Pauly Rodney
NH Constituency Organizer, Edwards campaign

There's a point in the course of the race that I think anyone working on a campaign reaches at least once. When you're at a speech or a rally and you've made a thousand calls, worked the reporters, pushed the angle, built the crowd, carefully laid the backdrop, and all your efforts are finally reduced to simply yelling and cheering as loud as you can when your guy walks in the room. For a moment, you are convinced that the one extra cheer and added applause will make it into a perfect event.

For just a moment, you aren't a planner or an organizer or a strategist or a spokesperson—you're just a person cheering your heart out for someone you believe in. It's a special moment, and it makes all the headaches and stress and hours and craziness of campaign life worth it, tenfold.

—Colin Van Ostern
NH Press Secretary, Edwards campaign

I sent this letter to someone back home this morning:
You say you understand, but I'm not sure you do. I don't know that it's something you can understand without being here in my shoes. What I do is more than a job for me, more than a resume builder, more than a path to success or some illusive fame that few of us campaign staff ever see. It's not really about that; it's about a lot more for me.

So even though I grumble sometimes about the long hours or late-night meetings, it's a good-natured, stress-relieving grumble. No one works these hours for so little pay and so little gratitude from the public unless they're passionate about it. This is my passion. This is what drives me every day. I believe in what I'm doing; I believe in the man I'm working for. This is my service to my country, whether you believe in what I'm doing or not. And I get very little thanks for it. I get doors slammed in my face, phones hung up on me, cursed at, shot the finger, called disparaging names by people who don't know a thing about me and never will—most of them don't even know anything about my candidate, and many of them will never even vote one way or the other.

And even though I know that you don't want the same things that I want or believe in, know that all I'm asking for is sympathy at the end of the day and a little understanding of how important this is for me. Because when you attack what I do, you're attacking everything I'm fighting for, and you're attacking me.

—Claire Wilker
Volunteer/Intern Coordinator & Office Manager, Gephardt campaign

It's on my days off (as few and far between as they are!) that I realize how addicted I am to my job. I wake up late, around 8 am, and turn on the TV. I bypass MTV and E! and go straight to CNN. I'm obsessed with making sure I didn't miss anything during my night's sleep. I sit in my bed with my laptop running so I can check my work e-mail, and, most important, read the news clips I get sent every day. The sounds of CNN run in the background while I read. I really can't complain about this set-up. I *am* still in bed!

All of the errands I run on my day off seem to be dictated by my job. I get my oil changed and get a tune-up on my car so that I don't have to worry about it for the next two months of the campaign. I go to the grocery store, but I don't go to buy food for my apartment. I buy food for the office. The proof of my addiction comes after the errands are done.

I go into the office. Granted, I'm only there for two hours, tops, but most normal people would not even have the urge to go. I have to be sure that I'm caught up on things I need to have done and also make sure that I'm ready for tomorrow to happen. I don't want to walk into chaos.

I know that I'm going to sit in my office for the next two months dying for my next day off. I'll be exhausted and worn out and swear up and down that the next day I have off will be spent entirely in bed, but I'll be lying. I guess there's a reason they find people like me to work on campaigns. Sane people would not have the drive or energy to keep on going.

—Katie Kiernan
Southern NH Regional Field Director, Gephardt campaign

153

Our area organizers stand in living rooms across the state as spokespeople, as the face of the campaign for Governor Dean. They have to answer questions that are completely out of their control and make people think not just about the issues, but also about the real reasons they support candidates—likeability, courage, leadership, trust. All of these words are fueling our campaign because they are based on feelings. People are angry, and they are thirsty for someone who has the experience to really do something. It's about building leadership and teaching people how to build leadership.

There were times last week when the whole field team was running house meetings at the same time. That's pretty powerful to sit in a living room and think not only is this house meeting happening, and not only are six other house meetings happening in Manchester, but 25 others are also happening across the state, just tonight.

—Delana Jones
Manchester Regional Field Director, Dean campaign

The staffers have incredible ideas and huge amounts of energy—a kind of undisciplined smartness. The challenge is figuring out a way to provide them with enough structure so that their ideas can be focused to a good end and not squashed, which is what tends to happen in field organizing. Over the last 10 years, field work has not been very engaging. The typical campaign has become so much about pushing information out one way rather than about having conversations with people. Conversations and relationships are slower to develop and require more of an investment. You can't just look at it as spending money; you're investing in people. I think it's important to consider this in order to change the way we do politics in this country. It's ridiculous that we spend as much money as we do on elections and come out with so little at the end of each one. So, the idea of using the opportunity to train a whole new generation of political organizers and leaders is totally exciting.

—Karen Hicks
NH State Director, Dean campaign

I figure, if you're going to do something—particularly something so hard, so uphill, so important—make it your life. Yesterday a friend asked me why she doesn't see me out at night with everyone else, enjoying the fact that there are hundreds of young people here in New Hampshire for only a few more weeks. The answer is: When I look back on this campaign, it will not just be about the number of votes we get. It will also be about whether or not I tried as hard as I possibly could. I'm not going to look back and regret the days I worked 16 hours. I'm going to regret the days I didn't.

I watched *Lord of the Rings* a week or two ago. Throughout the movie are battle scenes where hundreds or thousands of soldiers, yelling and screaming, rush the field. The vast majority are met with a quick and gruesome death. Most days, I feel like one of those soldiers. You know the odds are overwhelming. You know that chances are, at the end of your run down the field, you meet a nasty end. And yet you pick up your sword and run into battle. Part of it is because you know that you are needed. Part of it is because no matter how steep the odds, you know there is a chance.

Most of the people rushing the field do die. It's not like they don't know that before they take the first step. But they do it anyway. And sometimes it makes a difference.

—Colin Van Ostern
NH Press Secretary, Edwards campaign

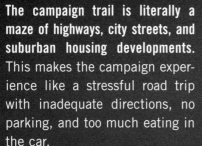

The campaign trail is literally a maze of highways, city streets, and suburban housing developments. This makes the campaign experience like a stressful road trip with inadequate directions, no parking, and too much eating in the car.

To cut down on the likelihood of accidents—which are nearly synonymous with campaigns—I instituted a new rule in the car. I am trying to limit myself to no more than two activities at once, in addition to driving. So, if I'm eating and following directions while driving, I can't use my phone. If I'm on the phone and following directions, I can't change CDs. If I'm eating and on the phone (which I shouldn't do anyway), I can't look at the directions. I just have to go straight until I get off the phone and evaluate where I am. I broke the rules all day today, but I'm going to get better.

—Kathy Roeder
NH Communications Director
Gephardt campaign

You must be the change you wish to see in the world.
—Mahatma Gandhi

FLOPHOUSING

IT IS CUSTOMARY FOR NEW HAMPSHIRE VOTERS TO HELP THE CAMPAIGN OF THEIR CHOICE BY PROVIDING HOUSING FOR THE LEGIONS OF OUT-OF-STATE STAFFERS, INTERNS, AND VOLUNTEERS.

If staffers are lucky, they end up in someone's guest room, but the latecomers inevitably end up in one of the many "crash pads" that spring up near the end of the campaign. These pads look a lot like the safe houses used by the mafia in the old days when the warring families would "go to the mattresses." A last resort is to find a dark corner at headquarters and roll out your sleeping bag after most of the staff goes home. This also requires membership in a local gym as you can only get by so long using the office sink for a shower.

I have always made it a point to open my home to the troops—the guest room, couches, sleeping bags on the floor. It's tough to say no to people who are so dedicated to a candidate that they put their lives on hold for a year to work 18-hour days, seven days a week, for wages that would make migrant farm workers strike.

One of my most memorable house guests was a young law school student who fit the above description to a T. He never complained, worked tirelessly, and defended his candidate fervently from even the slightest negative comment from a voter or opposing campaigner. A huge summer cookout for staff and supporters had yielded a large surplus of hot dogs and condiments, all of which ended up in my refrigerator. He wasn't home much over the next three months, but when he was, he would invariably be standing at the stove boiling up a couple of hot dogs. In the morning, he'd be slathering a couple of dogs with mustard and relish. At midnight, he'd be sitting in front of the TV, wiping mustard off of his mouth as he finished his late-night dinner.

In November, fearing that scurvy was setting in, the staff and I forced him to take the bus to his family's home for Thanksgiving. The staff was hoping that a day's worth of nutritious home cooking would give him the protein and vitamin infusion he so desperately needed. The trip was a nutritional success. Unfortunately he disrupted the family's festive spirit when he explained to his mother that he was so committed to his candidate that in the event of an assassination attempt, he would "take a bullet" for him. She cried for the entire day, begged him to return to law school, and then packed a turkey care package for his return trip to New Hampshire.

WILL KANTERES

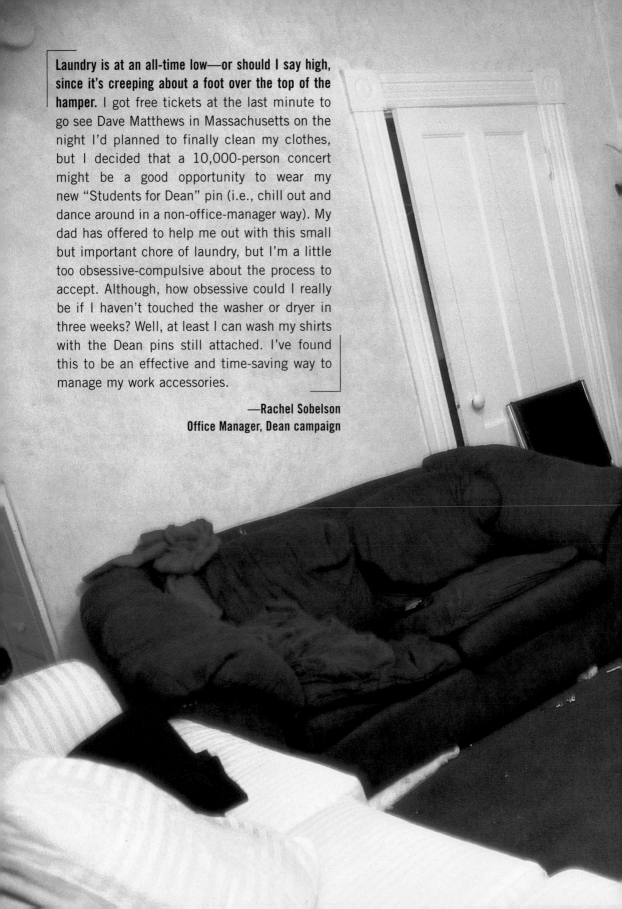

Laundry is at an all-time low—or should I say high, since it's creeping about a foot over the top of the hamper. I got free tickets at the last minute to go see Dave Matthews in Massachusetts on the night I'd planned to finally clean my clothes, but I decided that a 10,000-person concert might be a good opportunity to wear my new "Students for Dean" pin (i.e., chill out and dance around in a non-office-manager way). My dad has offered to help me out with this small but important chore of laundry, but I'm a little too obsessive-compulsive about the process to accept. Although, how obsessive could I really be if I haven't touched the washer or dryer in three weeks? Well, at least I can wash my shirts with the Dean pins still attached. I've found this to be an effective and time-saving way to manage my work accessories.

—Rachel Sobelson
Office Manager, Dean campaign

People need a release. You work all day, under stress and pressure that you cannot, for the most part, control. The campaign never goes away—it's in the news, on the TV. People everywhere know about it—relatives you hate, friends you love, people you went to high school with but have not seen in 10 years see you on C-Span. You make work calls at 11 o'clock at night and think it's normal. What we do is crazy. What happens in a single day is crazy. You need a release.

Sometimes, that release is simply going home and watching TV on your couch and not talking to anybody. I wake up nearly every morning thinking, "I can't wait to go back to bed tonight. I am tired, and I have a ton to do today. I love sleep. I can't wait to get that next six hours of sleep in." Sometimes I actually do go straight home at day's end.

More often than not, though, at the end of the day I just want to have fun for an hour or two and not think about work. Plus, I am usually wired to the gills. Hence, the bar. You get to see everyone on the other campaigns, and they are going through the same shit you are. You don't have to talk about it—it is understood. Their life is consumed by the same shit yours is, but for that one or two hours when you drink, smoke, gossip, and play, you forget that you left all your friends, forget that you left your home, forget that you never talk to your friends, forget that it is only Tuesday, forget the fact that it's only Tuesday is irrelevant anyway because you work seven days a week.

Forget the bad, talk about the good, and remember where you are. Remember what you are doing means something; think about how you will remember it in the years to come; think about the friendships you build along the campaign trail. And try to get members of the opposite sex to engage in "mutual campaign therapy"—all in some bar you probably would never go to in your home town but love and will love 'til the end.

That's a release. That's why people on campaigns do it—from the shy to the outgoing, doesn't matter, you've got to have a release.

—Theo Yedinsky
NH Political Director, Kerry campaign

This isn't the kind of job you can easily forget about, but it's healthy to try and get away from it sometimes. Maybe it's not so healthy to do that by drinking Bud Light, but it's hard to go hiking or do something truly healthy at 10 pm on a Wednesday when all the restaurants are closed and if I went to a movie I would just fall asleep. During the day it is difficult to step back and recalibrate to the point where I can think the election doesn't matter and I should just be happy that I'm healthy and that I have my family. Right now the election *really* matters. But when I'm hanging out with my friends the election fades and once again, the most important things in life become money for the jukebox, who's getting the next round, and laughing about how we all ended up in Manchvegas.

—Kathy Roeder
NH Communications Director, Gephardt campaign

Two K/Cristinas, six Davids, and two campaign dogs—this place is a regular circus! People are constantly in and out of the office. It is difficult to determine staff from the volunteers because both are growing at such a rapid pace. The "organized" chaos is evident everywhere. As we move into the final 40 days— less than 1,000 hours until voters go to the polls—the momentum is in full swing, and the excitement is contagious.

General Clark just finished a four-day swing through the state and was well received at each stop. The press attended the events and actually managed to write mostly favorable things—a successful trip.

Not to say that it wasn't without its blunders—far from it. The worst moment in the campaign was when a reporter was left behind, stranded on the side of the road in a town so small that it is barely registered on a map. And there was no cell-phone coverage in the area. So by the time he tracked someone down, his ride was 90 miles away. After much scrambling we sent a volunteer to rescue him. Needless to say, he was not a happy camper when he finally reached his destination.

It was by far, the worst moment on the campaign to date. New mandatory rule: All members of the traveling press must be accounted for at all times!

—Kristina Saunders
NH Deputy Communications Director, Clark campaign

It's almost 2 am. It's Christmas Eve. In four hours, I am scheduled to catch a flight back to Virginia so that I can see my family, none of whom I have seen in six months. I haven't yet packed my luggage. And I am at the office, trying to recruit volunteers for General Wesley Clark. This is what they mean when they say that "Wesley Clark is playing catch-up" with the other campaigns.

—Chris Smith
State Canvass Director, Clark campaign

I didn't go home for Christmas, even though we had three days off and I could have probably squeezed it in. My best friend sent me a Christmas card: "I miss you like crazy and need to have your mordant wit and considerable thirst with me at Maduro [our favorite martini bar back home]." I missed him so much I nearly cried when I read his note.

It wasn't that I didn't want to see my family and friends. I do miss them. It's just that I was so tired. It all seemed too much: the thought of all that time in the airport and on the plane, and all the organized stuff to do with the family—multiple Christmas dinners with various family members, maybe church, meeting up with friends, time in the car. An image floated around in my head of an insurmountable mountain that left me feeling weak with exhaustion just thinking about it.

I've missed other Christmases—on the road or with a boyfriend's family. So I decided to stay in New Hampshire. And sleep. And I did sleep—12 hours a day, three days in a row. But I was homesick.

—Anna Landmark
NH Field Director, Gephardt campaign

New Year's was the last hurrah. It feels like we've been pampered lately. Then again, that sounds crazy to say since there were just three days out of the last 80 that I didn't physically come into the office.

I loved celebrating New Year's with so many different campaign staffs at the "Intercampaign Triste." We're all unsure of our future, a little nervous, hopeful, excited, stressed, and completely engrossed. Wishing others Happy New Year felt like I was saying more. Good luck, hang in there, enjoy this experience. 2004 is the year we've been working for. Go make it happen.

I don't know where July went. Or August. CNN still shows footage of Gephardt at the Milford Labor Day parade, surrounded by staff wearing T-shirts and parade-goers lounging in lawn chairs. Those days, it felt like the primary would never happen. Voters didn't want to talk about it; they kept complaining we were starting too early. Now the days slip away too fast.

—Kathy Roeder
NH Communications Director, Gephardt campaign

It's all going to be over so soon, and what my life has been for more than 18 months will be no more. I think the reality of that finally hit me today. I felt paralyzed. I love it here. For all the exhaustion and frustration, this has been the most amazing experience of my life. Never before have I felt fundamentally changed by something—not a relationship, not a job, not a trip, not a book, not a class—I can't explain how I am different; I can just feel that I am.

And it's ending. In two more weeks, people whom I've worked with, played with, cried with, fought with, laughed with, shared beds and successes and meals and failures and countless bottles of wine with, will be flung across the country. People I've learned to lean on for everything will be thousands of miles away. It's amazing how intense relationships become when you spend 18 hours a day together, when you are so bound by a common cause, when others' highs and lows mirror your own.

January 27, 2004. The date has always been there. Like graduation day when you're a freshman, it just felt like it would never get here. You have fun along the way, you learn what you can, but it really never seems to get any closer. It's just always there—looming in the distance—always in the background at backyard parties, senior staff meetings, wiffleball games, bus tours, town halls, Friday night dinners—and now it's right around the corner.

I almost feel like I shouldn't sleep so that I can soak up every minute, every feeling. I know for certain that, looking back, I will romanticize this time in my life. I will remember glowingly the overwhelming sense of community, not the staff bickering; the common purpose, not the conflicting egos; the exhilaration, not the exhaustion; the responsibility, not the resentment at neglecting the rest of my life.

I'm pretty sure I'll do this again. I don't know that I'll be able not to.

—Meghan Scott
NH Trip Director, Edwards campaign

Dissent, rebellion, and all-around hell-raising remain the true duty of patriots.
—Barbara Ehrenreich

PYNX, NEW HAMPSHIRE

An increasing number of voters became intent on thoroughly vetting all the candidates before pledging to support any one of them. The best method for campaigns to accommodate these voters remained good old-fashioned "retail politics." But by the summer of 2003, efforts to reach voters transitioned from the traditional "mom and pop store" scale to the "regional mall" scale. The number of guests attending events began to swell into the hundreds—250 in Concord, 700 in Portsmouth, 1,200 in Walpole (population 3,599!), 2,000 in Nashua. House parties gave way to town hall meetings that gave way to arena rallies with overflow crowds previously reserved for visiting, incumbent Presidents.

Size mattered, not so much as a benchmark of a successful event, but as a clear indication of the nationwide trend of increasing numbers of voters willing to become engaged in the electoral process.

It gradually became obvious that the state was heading for a record voter turnout. After months of intense scrutinizing, voters began to choose their candidates. Voter skepticism transformed into riotous enthusiasm.

Candidates were dropped like rock stars into revved-up crowds in private backyards, town halls, vaudeville-era theaters, and modern ice arenas. By January, some rallies were so wildly charged that they resembled a traveling wartime USO show. These lively events brought back images of Bob Hope and Joey Heatherton bounding out of an Army helicopter with a troupe of go-go dancers in the middle of a Southeast Asian jungle, all neatly transposed onto a backdrop of a quaint New England setting.

John Kerry did, in fact, campaign by helicopter, but only to cover more ground in less time. And a handful of entertainers did make the trek to New Hampshire, but they came more as concerned activists than as performers. Crowds and staff were inspired by the words of celebrities like singer/songwriter Carole King, Martin Sheen (New Hampshire's favorite son, President Bartlett on *West Wing*), filmmaker Michael Moore, and a skating squadron of former Boston Bruins.

As field staffs organized supporters and analyzed voter surveys from across the state, the sheer volume of data to reference and cross-reference necessitated hiring more techies. And as press cars were traded in for press vans that were then traded in for press buses, the number of staff required for the care and feeding of the media grew to levels greater than any previous primary. The televised debates drew media coverage from around the world—more than 400 credentials were handed out at the ABC News debate in Durham. Although the debates did provide a great opportunity for large audiences to compare the candidates, none offered the kind of moments that communications directors dream of— the Ronald Reagan knockout, "I'm paying for this microphone, Mr. Green," or Walter Mondale's "Where's the beef?" sound bite.

New Hampshire residents hone their political forum skills at annual town meetings and are fearless when questioning the candidates. By November, large crowds confronted candidates with questions covering a wide spectrum of topics. Beyond the usual realm of questions about health care, Social Security, jobs, the war, affirmative action, clean air, and water, there were questions about medical marijuana, animal cruelty, land mines, and rights of foreign combatants—no subject was left unexplored. Extreme accessibility to the candidates and the campaigns' attention to voters' concerns enhance the sense of obligation to participate and provide a unique sense of empowerment. As a result, New Hampshire's voter turnout consistently runs ahead of the national average.

I hope the crowds will continue to grow over the coming years. Ancient Greece faced a similar dilemma as the right to participate in early democracy was expanded to include more social classes. The public forums, known as the Ecclesia or the People's Assembly, convened in the Pynx, a large amphitheater on a hillside overlooking the Acropolis. The Council repeatedly increased the size of the stage and the seating capacity at the Pynx to allow for the additional citizen participation.

Public debate in America has expanded from the soapbox to radio airwaves to cable TV to Internet chat rooms and blogs. The challenge for New Hampshire campaigns will be to find ways of accommodating the increasing crowds without compromising the intimacy so vital to getting to know the candidates.

WILL KANTERES

On this date, one year ago, Joe Lieberman announced he was running for President. I packed my bags, rented a car, and moved to New Hampshire. Soon after, I hired Emily as my deputy. 12 months in New Hampshire. 365 days. Two winters! I have been away from my fiancée, my family, and my friends. At times I never thought it would end. But tonight, with 14 days left to determine whether this year concludes with an exclamation point or a whimper, it seems as if the primary has flown by. I have worked for someone that I believe in, someone I know would make an outstanding President, and I have experienced the New Hampshire primary in full. There were good days and there were bad days, and there will be more of both in the two short weeks ahead, but I am more excited by the process today than I was when it began. And, though my fiancée will kill me, I just may be persuaded to do this again.

—Peter Greenberger
NH State Director, Lieberman campaign

Every day things move faster. The correspondents on cable news are even talking faster. Their hourly reports crack me up. "This hour is just about like the last hour, except that it's an hour closer to caucus hour. Race is very close. Unbelievably close. Historically close. To wrap up: It's close, and we're another hour closer to caucus hour. Reporting live, from Iowa." All done in a breathless voice that strikes panic in me, just because they sound panicked. What do I get out of watching this? Basically, I get an update on the time.

—Kathy Roeder
NH Communications Director, Gephardt campaign

There is a very familiar feeling that you get when that first negative attack is launched against your candidate. It's almost like being hit in the stomach. And it doesn't matter how many times you've gone through it—the first time it happens, it just knocks the breath out of you. I remember a day in June when we got attacked by Gephardt, Kerry, and Sharpton, and I think even Kucinich attacked us. In many ways that was a great training day, because by the third or fourth attack, it stopped being something that stunned the system and became something that's just part of what happens in a day.

Dealing with the attacks is about getting accustomed to them, but it also must be about making sure that we respond and set the record straight. We need to provide people with a larger context explaining why this is happening and what's at stake, especially since so many of our supporters have not been involved before. I think people have been jarred by it all.

—Karen Hicks
NH State Director, Dean campaign

To be perfectly honest, I've never seen positive campaigning. It's getting worse of course, and I think it's ridiculous, but what affects me the most is that I'm very close with people from other campaigns. Negative campaigning feels like an attack on them, as well as their candidate, which is awkward. We're friends, and that's more real to me than what these candidates think about each other. I know my friends will be there for me tonight when I need them.

But, suddenly, there's a lot more at stake. It's strange, especially as the race is tightening up. People are hunkering down, closing off, getting more competitive. Before it was sort of like "Everyone vs. Dean," so we could joke about what was going on. But now it seems like some others are back in the mix, and everyone is kind of keeping to themselves.

—Emily Silver
NH Deputy State Director & Chief of Staff, Lieberman campaign

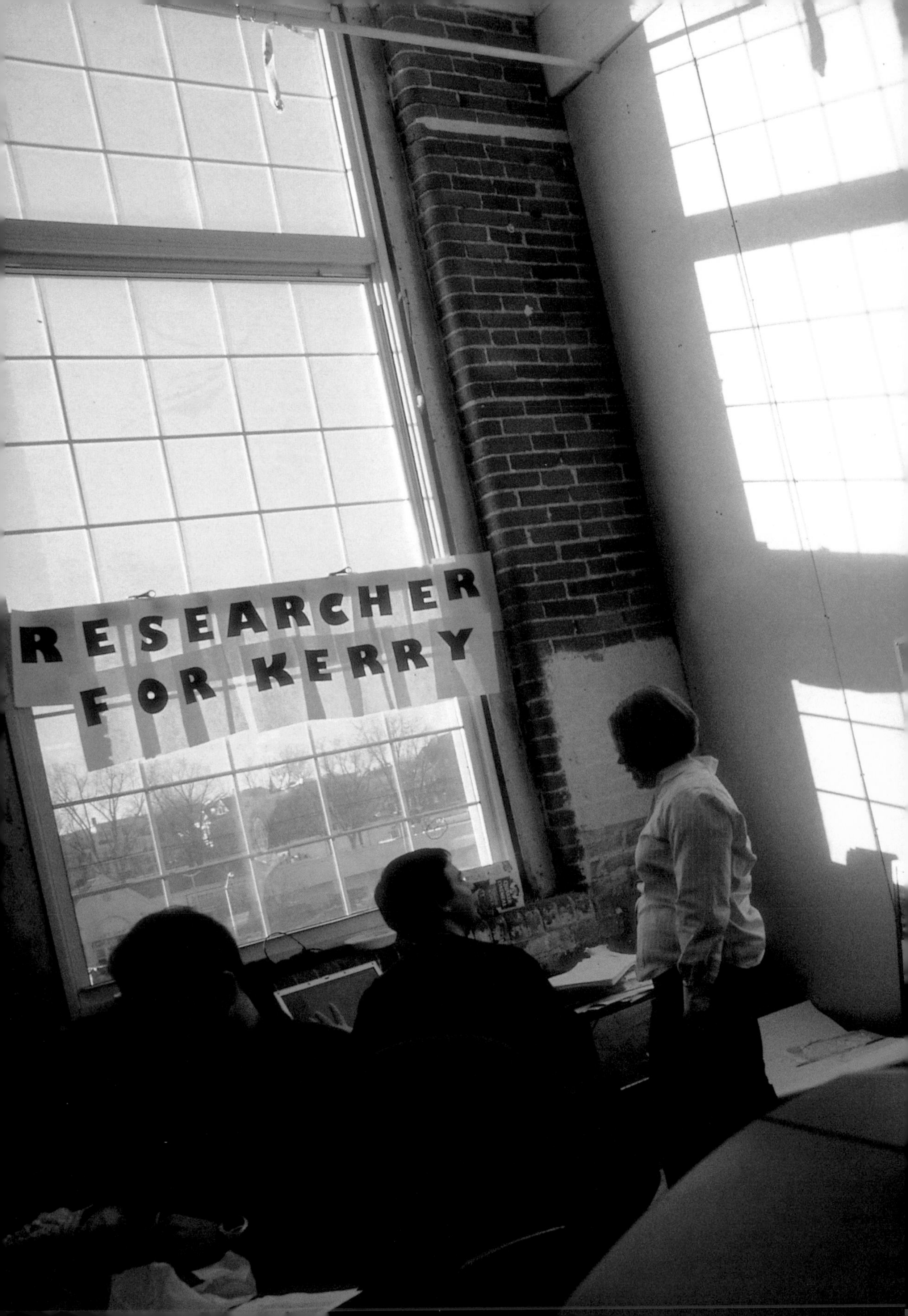
RESEARCHER
FOR KERRY

Waiting for the results of the Iowa caucuses is stomach-wrenching.
The polls there right now are so tight. Kerry could come in
first, or second, and come into New Hampshire with real
momentum, or he could come in fourth and we will have a
very sad last week here. This is even more of an emotional
roller coaster than other campaigns I've been involved with.
One of the staffers here yesterday said he was going to name
his firstborn child "Zogby" when yesterday's Zogby poll results
came out showing good things for Kerry.

—Judy Reardon
Senior Advisor, Kerry campaign

Howard
DEAN
for America
www.DeanForAmerica.com
Howard
DEAN
for America
www.DeanForAmerica.com
Howard
DEAN
Howard

For the longest time Election Day has been far off and the idea of winning, an abstract notion. Now, as we approach the end of all this, my assessment of how things will turn out seems to change every 15 minutes. We'll win, we'll lose, we'll win, we'll lose. I really don't know how to evaluate it all, even after all we did to get here.

—Karen Hicks
NH State Director, Dean campaign

I had a little bit of skepticism in my head. After all, nothing is ever guaranteed. Still I never quite pictured a crushing defeat for us in the Iowa race. At 7 pm I was still on top of the world. We were gonna win this thing, and if not a win, well, the stakes had changed so much in the past three days that a close second might not be as bad as previously thought, as long as we came in ahead of Dean. I checked the results almost every two minutes on the computer.

By 7:45 I had a sinking feeling, and by 8 I realized just how much the race had changed. Three days and the Iowa caucus had turned upside down. We only got 11 percent there, an upset I can't quite wrap my head around. Then again it's what the Iowa caucus is known for. How did Kerry and Edwards do it? Maybe the same way Gephardt did it in '88. But it doesn't matter when your heart is breaking.

Vultures. They came in so many forms, and so quickly too. The press already at our "victory party" had the decency to blend in and just type their stories, but then there were the ones who arrived later just wanting to take some pictures. Of what? Our tears, our heartbreak? Our supporters were not quite sure whether to stay or leave. Other campaigns, within an hour, asked us to join their staff. I got phone calls from people I'd never even met before: How would I like to work for so and so, or so and so?

All I wanted the press to do was leave. So I could cry. I refused to let them see me cry so they could get a picture or write about the "tearful staff." And when I had to pick up the phone and answer "Gephardt for President" as I had a hundred times a day, every day for eight months, I choked back the tears, answered the phone, and ran to the bathroom so no one saw me cry.

The tears came later. As I tore Gephardt signs off the office walls, as I packed up my crappy apartment that I had suffered living through just to work for a man I so desperately believed in. I saw the media converge for the final seven days—seven days I worked so hard for and endured so much for—those priceless last seven days that we would no longer be a part of. It's almost as if the city were screaming at me, "Gephardt . . . who?"

And so I cry for hours one night, 8, 9, 10, 11 pm. I cry until I fall asleep. And from then on, I feel an icy calm during the day as we pack, as I answer the phone, and cancel reservations for the week. I cry twice more as Dick Gephardt, a man I admire more than anyone else, breaks down during his withdrawal announcement when talking about his family. And I cry once more as I leave Manchester. It is done.

—Claire Wilker
Volunteer/Intern Coordinator & Office Manager, Gephardt campaign

This is a note I wrote to the Edwards field staff summing up how I feel about my experience in New Hampshire:

You guys should be so proud of yourselves. We have been the smallest and least funded field staff in the state for the last seven months, but we have risen and showed the country what determination and passion can accomplish.

Remember the early days last summer when we got "Edwards, who?" on the phones, and we all patiently explained that, in fact, the TV psychic was not running for President, and that, yes, we were calling on behalf of a US senator?

Remember those first crowds of a hundred people coming out to meet a guy they had never heard of and how hard we had to work to turn out those crowds? Remember those first few parades, when it was only us and we felt so small?

I know some may say all the magic and the mo' has happened since Iowa, but for me, it will always be those first few months. Before the commercials and media attention, when it was you guys, every day, fighting for the senator to be heard. It is because of all of you that we are where we are today. So stand up and be proud.

—Sarah Resnick
NH Deputy Field Director, Edwards campaign

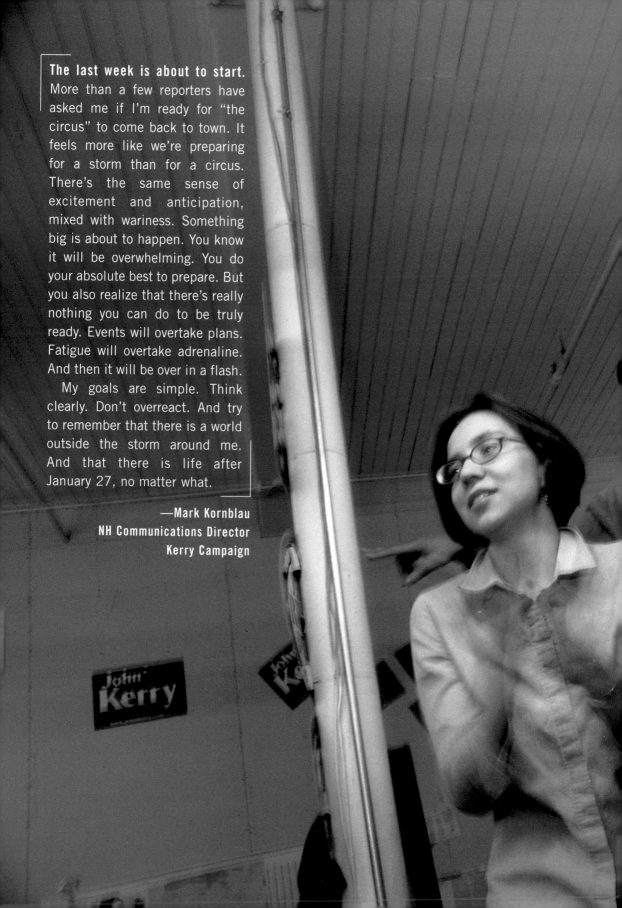

The last week is about to start. More than a few reporters have asked me if I'm ready for "the circus" to come back to town. It feels more like we're preparing for a storm than for a circus. There's the same sense of excitement and anticipation, mixed with wariness. Something big is about to happen. You know it will be overwhelming. You do your absolute best to prepare. But you also realize that there's really nothing you can do to be truly ready. Events will overtake plans. Fatigue will overtake adrenaline. And then it will be over in a flash.

My goals are simple. Think clearly. Don't overreact. And try to remember that there is a world outside the storm around me. And that there is life after January 27, no matter what.

—Mark Kornblau
NH Communications Director
Kerry Campaign

The day after the Iowa caucuses, all eyes turned to New Hampshire. Satellite trucks, buses converted into mobile studios, and cable news reporters clogged Elm Street overnight. Everywhere politics dominated the city. Through this media gauntlet I walked unnoticed into downtown thrift stores, offering our leftover office supplies and no-longer-needed furniture.

Shutting down our office a week before Election Day was a shock. The morning after Iowa, we had planned for Dick Gephardt's 3 am airport arrival and a downtown rally at 9 am. It was clear as soon as the results from the caucuses started coming in that we couldn't keep going with a fourth-place finish and that none of the New Hampshire campaign plans would happen. The charter jet left Iowa for St. Louis instead of New Hampshire.

I am so proud to have been a part of Dick Gephardt's campaign. But after almost a year of hard work, and at the climax of New Hampshire's political celebrity, we weren't even a part of the story.

—Kathy Roeder
NH Communications Director, Gephardt campaign

This is the most absurdly chaotic but exciting experience of my life. Our poll numbers have tripled in the past week, and so have our volunteers, our events, and everything else. My eyes are burning from fatigue, and even when I am in bed I can't sleep.

I feel like we went from riding a skateboard to driving a Ferrari. Two weeks ago we held a town hall meeting in Rochester and 100 people came. Yesterday we held a town hall meeting in Rochester and 1,000 people came. We are out of everything—literature, phone lists, yard signs. We have given it all away. We trained a dozen volunteers today to do press advance because we just have too much media for our staff to manage. It's amazing to watch the energy catch like a fire, watch it intensify as more people come together, and see how they feed off each other and how Edwards feeds off them. It doesn't feel contrived; it feels real. It really does feel like our time is now.

—Laura Memory Walters
NH Field Director, Edwards campaign

There is a fantastic adrenaline high that comes with total involvement in almost any kind of fast-moving political campaign—especially when you're running against big odds and starting to feel like a winner. For the same reason that nobody who has never come to grips with the spike can ever understand how far away it really is across that gap to the place where the smack junkie lives . . . there is no way for even the best and most talented journalist to know what is really going on inside a political campaign unless he has been there himself.
—Hunter S. Thompson, *Fear and Loathing: On the Campaign Trail*, 1973

LIGHTS, CAMERA, ACTION

MANCHVEGAS, MANCHGHANISTAN, MANCHUDISHU, RIO DE MANCHERO, MANCHANGELES.

Campaign workers use many names to describe Manchester, but on Election Day it is best known as the Center of the Universe. It is difficult to find more political junkies in one place at one time. There is no 12-step program for addiction to politics, so every four years the congregation of volunteers, pundits, reporters, national campaign staff, and operatives (present and past) grows exponentially. New Hampshire becomes the golden triangle for these junkies. It seems like there are more phone banks, rental vans, satellite trucks, visibility actions, pollsters, and talking heads in New Hampshire on Election Night than there are poppies in all of Cambodia, Laos, and Thailand.

Downtown Manchester takes on the feel of a Ringling Brothers circus. Live TV broadcasts are beamed up from specially fitted buses, sidewalk stand-ups, hotel lobbies, and City Hall. Documentary filmmakers, talk radio DJs, and CNN compete for set space at The Merrimack Restaurant (the center ring of campaign activity during the election). Consultants trade business cards as campaign staffers spin their message to reporters and to each other in the hotel lounge late at night. Print reporters outnumber voters and can be overheard interviewing their colleagues and swapping old war stories about this unique, quadrennial event.

You can almost hear the thunder of the 8.6 seismic shift in power.

Suddenly, the *Concord Monitor*'s editorial page wields a club equal in weight to that of *The New York Times*'. The usual suspects seated at the power tables of Washington and New York's haughtiest restaurants wait in line for breakfast at local diners. Legions of lobbyists, national fundraisers, and old friends of the candidates clog the private jet terminal at the local airport.

They all come to be a part of what for them is the pivotal moment—the vote tally on Election Night. But what they are seeing is one frame in a year-long movie. They may experience the headlines that grace the front pages of the Wednesday papers, but many leave without any sense of the countless human dramas that are the real story in any election. If you've never thrown your entire life into a campaign, you may find it difficult to imagine what a staffer is feeling as the curtain comes down on Election Night.

The activists of this year's campaigns deserved every one of the victory speeches that I heard on Election Night. They worked with unwavering passion. They gave it their best, and then some. They had nothing to concede. Those who shed tears will soon understand that they were disappointed but not defeated. And those who were elated will cherish their moment in history for a lifetime. All will wake up on the day after the election knowing that their work has just begun.

WILL KANTERES

John Kerry
PRESIDENT
www.JohnKerry.com
CLARK 04
FOR PRESIDENT
PRESID
clark04

John Kerry
PRESIDENT
www.johnkerry.com
John Kerry
PRESIDENT
www.JohnKerry.com
CONSERVATION VOTERS
ERRY
LEAGUE OF CONSERVATIO
KER

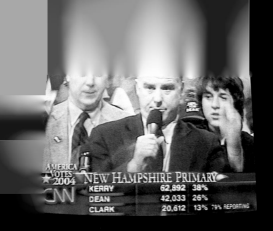

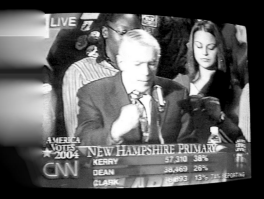

It was hard to keep my spirits up during the dark days when Kerry was was down in the polls, but I was motivated by the old hands on our team. Governor Shaheen and our senior advisor Sue Casey would say, "Anything can happen in the last couple of weeks of a campaign. You just don't know, so you have to keep trying, and never give up." And even in the darkest days, experienced politicians were signing up to support John Kerry. These are people who would never decide to sign on with a sure loser, and they were making the judgment that we could still do it.

When I got back to our headquarters from my own ward on Election Night, I joined the small group of staffers and volunteers who were taking in the election returns in our boiler room. Virtually every precinct came in better than we expected; where Kerry was winning, it was by wider margins than we had expected, and where we were not winning, it was by smaller margins than we expected. We cheered at 8:30 when CNN projected John Kerry the winner, and as returns continued to come in, we knew Kerry would win New Hampshire by double digits.

Hugging Nick Clemons and Ken Robinson, who had joined the campaign even earlier than I had, was very special. We had done it. By the time we felt we were ready to join the official party at the Center of New Hampshire, Kerry was soon going to take the stage for his victory speech. We didn't want to miss the speech, so we all watched together on the big-screen TV we had rented to watch the Iowa caucus results. We drank beer and champagne and cheered along with the crowd in the ballroom. And when it was done, we headed to the Rover, joining the staff and Governor Shaheen and a few supporters for a great, great celebration.

—Judy Reardon
Senior Advisor, Kerry campaign

LIVE

AMERICA
VOTES
2004

NEW HAMPSHIRE PRIMARY

EDWARDS	17,123	12%
LIEBERMAN	12,642	9%
KUCINICH	2,080	2%

71% REPORTING

NEW HAMPSHIRE
PRIMARY

KERRY WINNER	81,223	39%

EDWARDS	25,386	12%

DEAN	55,120	26%

LIEBERMAN	18,188	9%

CLARK	26,241	13%

CNN

96% REPORTING

How does winning feel? The answer is that it feels great to win, surreal. Winning the New Hampshire primary is one of those things that you never think will happen to you and then, one day, it does. You become "one of those people," for lack of a better way of putting it. It's a little overwhelming to think that all of the sacrifice and hard work paid off. It's an awesome feeling.

Honestly though, I can't help but feel that on January 27 I was in the right place at the right time—the intersection where risk, sacrifice, hard work, and luck meet. What I was doing four weeks before the election when we were down was not all that different from what we did the last week when we won. I worked harder than some, not as hard as others. I worked smarter than some, not as smart as others. Everyone took the risk to be here and everyone sacrificed—all the campaign staffers. The New Hampshire primary is tough. It's the best and worst thing I have ever done. I wouldn't trade the experience for anything.

—Theo Yedinsky
NH Political Director, Kerry campaign

John
Ke
PRESID
www.Iohnk
John

When we lost the primary, I felt as though I had been in a terrible accident. Governor Dean was supposed to win, the New Hampshire team was supposed to go on to other great contests, and I was supposed to feel as though I'd experienced the greatest accomplishment of my life. I have this scrapbook of experiences from the campaign that deserves a final photograph I fear I will never see.

For eight months I helped build an unbelievable grassroots structure. Like so many other campaign staffers, I worked like an architect, constructing an intricate sandcastle. At first we had nothing but the most basic tools: some sand, some ideas, and enough mortar to hold a few things together. By mid-January we were putting the finishing touches on something that was as beautiful as it was functional. When we lost, it was like a giant wave had taken it all away.

After the initial shock of second place, I looked around and I saw the foundations of the Dean campaign staring back. It wasn't beautiful or shiny, but it had all of the elements that brought me to the team in the first place.

I am a part of a community that is spread out around the United States. I am so proud of what we have done and so honored to have watched it happen in my backyard. I have made a difference.

—Rachel Sobelson
Office Manager, Dean campaign

So we won. We won New Hampshire, the greatest comeback ever. We won New Hampshire! Wahoo! We were down by over 30 points at one time, and we came back to beat our closest competition by double digits. It was our hopes and dreams come true. But really, who would have thought? If there ever comes a point in my life when I'm involved in something that I begin to doubt, all I will have to do is think about the past nine months and remember that anything is possible! I have been on board since early last year, experiencing all the ups and downs. So for me, the victory is that much sweeter.

The day after the election everyone seemed to move in a bit of a fog . . . until we got our marching orders. Before I knew it, I had moved out of the office and my apartment and was on my way to DC, leaving New Hampshire behind. It was by far the experience of a lifetime! Thanks, John Kerry, for an amazing ride!

—Johanna Voss
Statewide Volunteer/Intern Coordinator, Kerry campaign

Needless to say, it's been a whirlwind. The New Hampshire John Kerry for President HQ went from having more people than we could ever possibly handle— volunteers, staff, surrogates, late-arriving help in the final days leading up to the election—to being empty and deserted, all within a 24-hour period. Our New Hampshire win required the immediate dispatch of all staff, leaving the junky furniture, rented computers, phones, office equipment, food, trash, chum, and everything else under the sun to clean itself up. The original "crew," Ken Robinson, Judy Reardon, Pat Morris, Kate Murphy, Nick Clemons, and me, were the six left to deal with what was remained, to finish what we had started almost a year earlier . . . and a long year it was. We had energy from the extraordinary weeks leading up to our success on January 27, but the energy was also accompanied by utter exhaustion and the bigger task that lay ahead, as we, too, were dispatched to continue the good fight.

—Jessie Grant
NH Director of Operations, Kerry campaign

Election Day: The fat lady sang, and everyone heard her. The thing about campaigns is that there's not much difference between second and last place, especially when you're "supposed" to win. I'm pretty tired now and I'm not in the best mood, but there are a few things that help cushion the blow of the loss: I believed in myself and my choice to work for Governor Dean. Since the campaign began, I've been surrounded by people with uncompromising values and a relentless determination for change. Our organization was brilliantly executed, and we did what we set out to do. Our determined volunteers helped make that possible and sacrificed as much as any staffer during the campaign. It's going to be tough to walk away from our supporters who didn't just believe in Dean but believed in all of us as a team. That's something for which I'll always be grateful.

Even as I write this, there's a part of me that doesn't want the campaign to be over. Yes, that includes the 18-hour days, seven days a week, the annoying novella-length e-mail questions that you get from a supporter you briefly met, the practical jokes at the office (and there were many), the one bathroom for at least 60 people, the fact that I drank more coffee than I put gas in my gas tank, and, yes, losing.

—Steve Gerencser
NH Deputy Political Director, Dean campaign

There's an expression in sports about "leaving it all on the field." The idea is that when you walk back into the locker room, you should barely be able to stand. I think that's true for campaigning. In the final days of a campaign, most people are at the very edge (or past the edge) of healthy lifestyles. Many have put on or lost a lot of weight; a lot of relationships are stressed; a lot of friendships are on pretty rocky ground after months of neglect. A guy I worked for in the last election told me a story about how his wife was reading his young daughter a children's book about a family of bears, and when she got to the part where the father bear came home after work, the girl broke down crying.

So why do we do this? I have to steal a line from my boss to explain it: Because cynics didn't build this country. Optimists did. And because I believe in the politics of what's possible.

Through the past year and through this campaign, I have learned two great lessons: There will always be heartache and struggle; and people of strong will can make a difference. One is a sad lesson; the other is inspiring. I choose to be inspired.

—Colin Van Ostern
NH Press Secretary, Edwards campaign

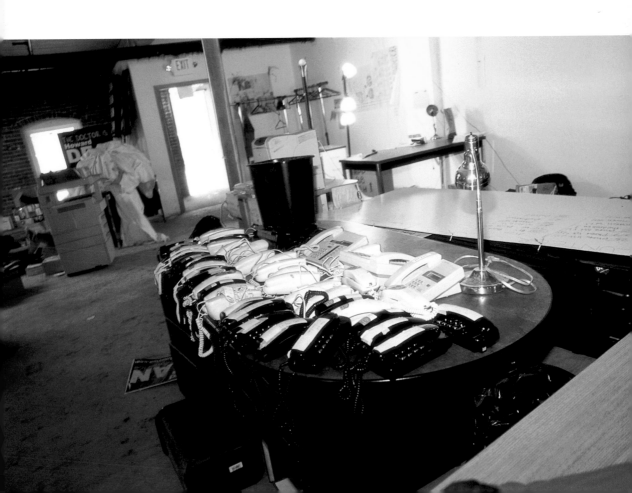

As the election got closer and closer, forces bigger than our organization came up on the horizon, almost like a weather system that we had absolutely no control over—the increased scrutiny of the media, the attacks from the other campaigns. There was a big shift probably 10 or 15 days before the election where you could literally feel it slipping away. This vessel we had created was suddenly taking on a lot of water. There was all this momentum, but it was moving in the wrong direction for us.

Had we held onto our lead in Iowa, had we not had Dean's "scream" speech, we would have spent more time using our resources to reach out and connect to the people who hadn't made up their minds yet. Instead, we spent all our time post-Iowa shoring up our supporters. The whole final week was a struggle, both to keep Governor Dean mentally in the game and to keep all the organizers on a path that was plausible. Because we knew our supporters, we were able to activate our social networks, bringing people back and making up 14 points in the polls in a single week. Our base of support had deep roots. Without those roots, the storm would have just blown us out of the water, scattering everything that we had done to the winds. We turned out our "ones" [solid supporters] on Election Day, but for us the problem was twofold: The turnout was 40 percent higher than even the secretary of state projected, which made our work smaller; and the people who made up their minds during the last month didn't come our way—at all.

I feel like at some level I let the staff down because we had created this whole strategy and told them that if you build this new model, we will succeed. Those of us in the leadership of the campaign and Howard Dean share a lot of the blame for the loss. There was this inconsistency because we told them all along that they had the power, but they actually didn't have the power to overcome what was happening. Somebody had moved the goal post. Our staff did everything better than I could have imagined. I've lost before, but most of them haven't. It's devastating. It's just devastating.

But I also know that they've all had this unbelievable experience. We started out with the premise that every single person matters. Had we not built the campaign this way, it would have been more devastating. It's not like our team worked harder than any other team. Everybody put the same thing into it, but for our team, there was a whole different set of rewards which came out of trying something different. They learned and grew and developed in ways that are separate from winning and losing. We created structures and resources that don't just go away when the circus leaves town. The team we built during this campaign will be lifelong organizers and will continue the work we started here.

—Karen Hicks
NH State Director, Dean campaign

As fate would have it, the prize of the Democratic nomination seems to have been awarded in Iowa. Which places all of us who battled so bravely in New Hampshire in a position all too unsettling. What happened to the ornery Granite Stater of primaries past who greeted the results from Iowa with an upturned nose and a contrarian vote? Why did we spend all this time in drudgery, in cold and gray New Hampshire?

Since New Hampshire's completion, with things ending much as they began a year before, I have pondered that terrible, fatuous question: "What did it all mean?" I have no easy answer. A week before Iowa, Clarkies intently watching polling trends were convinced that General Clark was on the cusp of a great wave of success. Oh, the crowds we had! Of course, that great wave turned out to have another candidate's name on it. Senior campaign officials repeatedly told us that we needed only to "get our ticket punched" in New Hampshire in order to later harvest electoral rewards. But then, that piece of the Clark scenario fell through as well. Delicately and beautifully, they were stacked on one another, but when they fell—our articles of faith in the primary process, our illusions—they came down hard and ugly.

No, New Hampshire did not fail us, nor, by the way, did we fail New Hampshire. New Hampshire delivered, in full and in maverick style, a completely unpredictable finish. And we faithful winter soldiers produced the largest Democratic primary turnout in the history of the state.

—Chris Smith
State Canvass Director, Clark campaign

It has been a bumpy few weeks, and I am not at all sure of what lies ahead. Surprisingly, I have remained fairly calm and remarkably positive. In New Hampshire I had a job I loved so much that it didn't seem like work. I was surrounded by brilliant and generous colleagues who gave me trust, respect, and decision-making power every day. I made meaningful friendships in New Hampshire that I will take with me everywhere. I found an energy and strength within myself that I didn't know existed.

But most important and most sincerely, I fought like hell for a man I truly believed in. Joe Lieberman is smart, direct, tough, fair, decent, and kind. He gives new meaning to the word integrity. I have never met anyone I respect more. Simply put, Joe Lieberman is the best President we never had. Moving to New Hampshire to work for him is one of the best decisions I've ever made. I know it, I'm proud of it, and it changed my life. I think I'll be OK.

—Kristin Carvell
NH Press Secretary, Lieberman campaign

Some of the people I became closest with in New Hampshire were from outside my own campaign. Now that the primary is over, there is a difficult, if understandable, distance between us. In New Hampshire we shared a lot of the same experiences—the fatigue, the isolation, the never-ending work hours—but now it seems like we aren't all on the same page. Some of us are disappointed; some of us are celebrating. Some are excited about new positions and new states we are being sent to, and others are dealing with defeat. These results, unlike poll numbers, have such definitive consequences that they entwine the personal and the professional more closely than before.

—Laura Memory Walters
NH Field Director, Edwards campaign

My heart was utterly broken. I worked for 10 months on the New Hampshire primary, and we were beaten badly. I will never regret my decision to work for Joe Lieberman because I still believe that of all the candidates in the race, he is the most genuine, honest, decent individual and probably the one best equipped to reach out to Republicans and Independents. First the press, then the voters, disagreed.

Overworked and exhausted, the staff was sent roaring to sharp peaks and freefalling into bottomless lows. When the Iowa results rolled in, there was a funereal atmosphere in the office—everyone sulked, and people were paralyzed at their desks. But by the end of that final week, we had dug down deep, spurred on by the ever-positive Joe Lieberman himself. We even claimed to have "Joe-mentum." In retrospect, we had little momentum, but the thought at least allowed the staff and volunteers to continue fighting.

Primary night was one of the most difficult nights of my life. It was obvious from the first results that things were not going to turn out as we had hoped. It would have been easy to simply call it a night, head home, and catch up on some much needed sleep. But there was a party and there was media waiting and the candidate had to speak, so we all paraded over to hear him.

I knew Lieberman was soon going to be out of the race after his New Hampshire finish. John Kerry was launched by the Granite State on his way to the nomination. Now, with my candidate out of the hunt, it's actually pretty easy for me to say that I am a Kerry supporter. In the end, I think New Hampshire voted based on the desire for someone, anyone, to beat Bush. That was precisely why I supported Lieberman, and the strength of that feeling now compels me to support the candidate who will be our nominee, the man with the best shot at taking down Bush, Senator Kerry.

—Christopher Pappas
NH Deputy Field Director, Lieberman campaign

DEMOCRACY WASN'T BUILT IN A DAY

NOT UNTIL 508 BC DID CLEISTHENES, BUILDING ON THE FOUNDATION OF THE LAWS ENACTED BY SOLON IN THE PREVIOUS CENTURY, SET ATHENS ON THE PATH TOWARD CREATING HISTORY'S FIRST DEMOCRATIC SOCIETY.

In what could be described as the first recorded case of gerrymandering, Cleisthenes restructured the aristocratic Council, doubling the number of citizens eligible to participate in the governing of Athens. He divided the population into ten tribes rather than four, and realigned the constituents from each of the city's three districts. Thus, he dissolved the power of the ruling clans and created a broader, more representative power structure. The constant struggle between the oligarchic and democratic forces continued for nearly two hundred years (some would say that it continues even today). Forever a work in progress, the one constant tenet of democracy through the ages has been the fundamental duty of all eligible citizens to participate in the democratic process.

Citizens in ancient Greece looked down upon those who neglected their duty and branded them as *idioitis*—the Greek root of the modern word "idiot." The original use of this word was as a derogatory term that disparaged more than a person's intellectual ability. As an honor to those who refuse to be idiots, and with apologies to Homer, I respectfully submit a lyric tribute to the foot soldiers of democracy:

The ancient Greeks would be relieved
to see democracy which they conceived
in marble forums 'neath the golden sunlight
being kept alive by staffers in a state of granite.

The system works but not yet to perfection,
need I remind you of the Florida election?
But it is you who brave low temps and low wages,
forgo sleep and food to leave your mark on history's pages.

You toil to save us from what the gods must have known,
that tricks of the trade would one day have grown
from black marbles, clay ostraka, and Trojan horses
to robocalls, hanging chads, and unnamed sources.

'Tis a duty of all citizens to serve in the political arena
But you, O Sons of Pericles and Daughters of Athena,
whether in the house of Field, Advance, IT, or Press,
are the souls with whom our democracy's future rests.

Your talents, like a musician's timing and a poet's rhyming,
cannot be understood without Mt. Olympus first climbing.
Your inspiration is a gift from the mythic political muse
and rises to protect us all from fascist rulers and Fox News.

Praise to the chosen ones whose blood boils with passion—
May this book honor your work, your mark, your fashion.
The Odyssey brings you here and takes you away;
your blood, sweat, and tears bring us hope on Election Day.

—WILL KANTERES

NAME, RANK & SERIAL NUMBER

PAGE NUMBERS IN BOLD INDICATE WHERE PHOTOGRAPHS OF PROJECT PARTICIPANTS APPEAR.

MARC BARANOV, 24, Tarazana, CA, Dean campaign Nashua Regional Field Director; previously worked as a field organizer on Paul Wellstone's 2002 campaign. **p. 69**

RAYMOND "Chairman" BUCKLEY, 44, Manchester, NH, Lieberman campaign Eastern Regional Political Director; NH House Minority Whip; ninth Presidential campaign. **pp. 62; 71**

KRISTIN "Soft Serve" CARVELL, 29, North Augusta, SC, Lieberman campaign Press Secretary; five-year press secretary veteran; first NH Primary. **pp. 60; 62; 90**

CALEB CLARK, 28, Portsmouth, NH, Edwards campaign NH Deputy State Director; worked on the 2000 & 2002 Martha Fuller Clark for Congress campaigns in NH prior to the 2004 primary. **p. 79**

NICK "Nikita Clementine" CLEMONS, 30, Portsmouth, NH, Kerry campaign NH Field Director; worked as a Nashua field organizer in his first NH Primary in '96 for President Clinton; later worked on three Jeanne Shaheen campaigns. **p. 37; 94; 140-141**

YONI "Yo-Co" COHEN, 22, Lexington, MA, Dean campaign Salem/Derry Regional Field Director; first campaign as a paid staffer.

MATTHEW "Old School" GARDNER, 29, Glenely, MD, Dean campaign NH Press Secretary; quit his job at a DC law firm to join the Dean team.

STEVE GERENCSER, 30, Cheshire, CT, Dean campaign NH Deputy Political Director; worked for VT Sen. Patrick Leahy; later worked in the 2002 NH Senate race. **pp. 16-17**

JESSIE GRANT, 25, Exeter, NH, Kerry campaign NH Director of Operations; worked for Jeanne Shaheen campaign and administration; first Presidential primary. **pp. 22; 58; 84; 116; 208**

ERIK GREATHOUSE, 31, Calena, AL, Gephardt campaign NH State Director; has worked in electoral politics for nearly a decade, though this was his first NH primary. **p. 86; 88**

PETER "Greeny" GREENBERGER, 30, New York, NY, Lieberman campaign NH State Director; third tour of duty in NH Primary politics. **pp. 14; 35; 143; 165**

KAREN "Kicks" HICKS, 34, Concord, NH, Dean campaign NH State Director; first Presidential campaign; previously worked as Political Director for Jeanne Shaheen's Senate and gubernatorial races; has been organizing for over 14 years. **pp. 40; 48; 71; 72; 74; 96; 115; 166; 215**

TOM HUGHES, 34, Norwich, VT, Dean campaign NH Field Director; has a long history of working advance on Presidential campaigns; was the Executive Director of the VT Democratic Party before coming to NH to work on the 2004 primary. **pp. 24; 45**

DELANA "Diesel" JONES, 24, Harrison, AR, Dean campaign Manchester Field Director; learned NH politics while working on the 2002 election cycle in NH. **pp. 13; 64-65; 68; 115; 125; 166**

KATIE KIERNAN, 22, Bedford, NH, Gephardt campaign Southern NH Regional Field Director; first worked in NH politics during the 2002 Martha Fuller Clark for Congress campaign.

MARK "O.G." KORNBLAU, 28, New York, NY, Kerry campaign NH Communications Director; has worked with the political media since 1988; first time working the NH primary.

BEN "I don't have time for this" LaBOLT, 22, La Grange, IL, Dean campaign Seacoast Regional Field Director; came to the campaign just a few hours after his college graduation. **p. 171**

ANNA "Banana" LANDMARK, 25, Mount Horeb, WI, Gephardt campaign NH State Field Director; has worked on eight campaigns; was drawn to Gephardt partly due to her labor-union work. **p. 153; 187**

MIKE MATTOON, 27, Belleville, NJ, Gephardt campaign Deputy Field Director & Labor Coordinator; worked with Gephardt in Washington before joining the NH Primary team. **pp. 4; 38; 102-103; 122; 153**

KRISTYN McLEOD, 25, Franconia, NH, Edwards campaign NH Political Director; first interacted with NH voters as field coordinator during the 2000 Jeanne Shaheen for Governor race. **pp. 125; 138**

ROBBY "Mookie" MOOK, 23, Norwich, VT, Dean campaign Deputy Field Director/GOTV Director; first worked for Dean during his 1998 campaign for governor. **pp. 115; 166**

COLIN VAN OSTERN, 24, Concord, NH, Edwards Campaign NH Press Secretary; was the press secretary for two statewide races, including Jeanne Shaheen for Senate, prior to this campaign. **p. 125**

CHRISTOPHER PAPPAS, 23, Manchester, NH, Lieberman campaign NH Deputy Field Director; NH State legislator; began working in campaigns in 1996. **p. 62**

JUDY REARDON, 45, Manchester, NH, Kerry campaign NH Senior Advisor; was a NH state representative from 1985-1989; served as legal counsel to Gov. Jeanne Shaheen for six years. **p. 50**

SARAH "The Funnel" RESNICK, 25, Chicago, IL, Edwards campaign Deputy Field Director; first canvassed at age five for the Mondale-Ferraro campaign. **p. 93** (r-bottom)

PAULY RODNEY, 26, Vineland, NJ, Edwards campaign NH Constituency Organizer; found his first NH primary a great place to apply his political degree. **p. 151**

KATHY "Roed-Rules" ROEDER, 28, Carmichael, CA, Gephardt Campaign NH Communications Director; planted her first lawn sign in 1992 for Clinton/Gore in CA. **pp. 101; 122; 128; 172; 186; 192**

KRISTINA SAUNDERS, 26, Albuquerque, NM, Graham campaign NH Deputy Press Secretary & Clark campaign NH Deputy Communications Director; came to NH in 2002 for the governor's race; returned for 2004 NH primary. **p. 168**

MEGHAN SCOTT, 23, Emmaus, PA, Edwards campaign NH Trip Director; worked on Caroline McCarley's Senate campaign in 2002, stayed in NH to work on the primary. **pp. 64-65; 98; 139**

EMILY "MLE" SILVER, 24, Amherst, MA, Lieberman campaign NH Deputy State Director & Chief of Staff; first Presidential campaign; worked in campaign finance before coming to NH. **pp. 71; 113**

JAMAL SIMMONS, 32, Detroit, MI, Graham & Clark campaigns Traveling Press Secretary; over 10 years of media experience; first NH primary. **p. 82**

CHRIS "Smithers" SMITH, 24, Alexandria, VA, Graham campaign Manchester Field Director & Clark campaign State Canvass Director; fourth campaign as field organizer; first NH Primary. **p. 146**

RACHEL "the Sobs" SOBELSON, 19, Concord, NH, Dean campaign Office Manager; began campaigning at age 12; took off a year of college to work on the NH primary. **p. 93; 200; 207**

JOHANNA "Jojo" VOSS, 24, Mattaporsett, MA, Kerry campaign Statewide Volunteer/Intern Coordinator; found Kerry through environmental activism at the University of Oregon; first NH primary. **p. 191**

LAURA "Hot Date" MEMORY WALTERS, 28, Greensboro, NC, Edwards campaign NH Field Director; braved the cold to experience the NH primary for the second time in 2004; worked for Al Gore for President in the previous cycle. **pp. 98; 165**

CLAIRE "Steel" WILKER, 21, Citrus Springs, FL, Gephardt campaign Volunteer/Intern Coordinator & Office Manager; left college in Florida to work in NH. **pp. 89; 153**

THEO "Breadislav Dogdinsky" YEDINSKY, 32, Devon, PA, Kerry campaign NH Political Director; longtime Democratic Party operative; first Presidential primary. **pp. 121; 137; 165; 208**

PHOTO INDEX

Front Cover: Connecticut Sen. Joe Lieberman giving his stump speech at a house party at the home of Katrina and Dick Swett, Bow; **pp. 4-5** Mike Mattoon, first staffer for Missouri Rep. Richard Gephardt hired in NH, working into the night at a supporter's law office in Manchester's millyard; **pp. 8-9** Staffer Aaron Holmes accompanying then Vermont Governor Howard Dean during an early NH visit; **p. 10** Visibility outside the NH Democratic State Committee Jefferson-Jackson fundraising dinner, Center of New Hampshire, Manchester; **p. 13** Dean campaign's Manchester Field Director Delana Jones at an early-morning rally, Executive Court Conference Center, Manchester; **p. 14** State Director Peter Greenberger working from his small downtown Manchester apartment before the Lieberman campaign HQ opened; **pp. 16-17** NH Deputy Political Director Steve Gerencser working out of his girlfriend's grandmother's house in Manchester before the Dean campaign HQ opened; **pp. 18-19** Setting up the state HQ for Massachusetts Sen. John Kerry, Manchester; **pp. 20-21** Painting the Lieberman HQ, Manchester; **p. 22** Director of Operations Jessie Grant setting up the Kerry HQ, Manchester; **p. 23** Telephone orientation for the staff at the state HQ of North Carolina Sen. John Edwards, Manchester, NH; **pp. 24-25** NH Field Director Tom Hughes during the first night at the Dean HQ, Manchester; **p. 26 & 29** Visibility outside the NH Democratic State Committee fundraising dinner, Manchester; **pp. 30-31** State Democratic Party convention, Derryfield School, Manchester, NH; **p. 32** Preparing for an outdoor town hall event, downtown Manchester; **p. 33** Florida Sen. Bob Graham staffer David Moore setting up the room, University of New Hampshire, Durham; **pp. 34-35** Peter Greenberger (center) standing with fellow staffer Joe Eyer and AP photographer Jim Coles during a diner stop with Joe Lieberman, Chez Vachon, Manchester, NH; **pp. 36-37** NH Field Director Nick Clemons mapping out his plan, Kerry HQ, Manchester; **pp. 38-39** Gephardt campaign's Mike Mattoon canvassing Manchester's East Side; **p. 40** Howard Dean is guided through his "call time" by NH State Director Karen Hicks and other staffers, Center of New Hampshire, Manchester; **p. 42** David Moore awaiting the arrival of his candidate, Bob Graham, Robie's Country Store, Hooksett; **pp. 44-45** Tom Hughes awaiting the arrival of his candidate, Howard Dean, SEE Science Center, Manchester; **pp. 46-47** Aide to Rev. Al Sharpton listening to his speech during the annual NH State Democratic Party's Jefferson-Jackson fundraising dinner, Center of New Hampshire, Manchester; **p. 48** Karen Hicks mapping out the campaign's growth, Dean HQ, Manchester; **p. 49** Kerry team hard at work, Kerry HQ, Manchester; **pp. 50-51** Senior Advisor Judy Reardon in her office, Kerry HQ, Manchester; **p. 52** Manchester Field Director Kate Murphy signing in volunteers for orientation during the first large Kerry canvass, Kerry HQ, Manchester, NH; **p. 53** Kerry HQ, Manchester; **p. 57** Office Manager Wade Chappell at work in the Edwards HQ, Manchester; **p. 58** Jessie Grant (l) working with a volunteer, Kerry HQ, Manchester; **p. 59** Staffers at lunchtime, Kerry HQ, Manchester; **p. 60** Press Secretary Kristin Carvell during a scheduling meeting, Lieberman HQ, Manchester; **p. 62** (l-r) Volunteer Coordinator Meagan Coffman, NH Press Secretary Kristin Carvell, Eastern Regional Political Director Raymond Buckley, Manchester Field Coordinator Tom Petrillo, and NH Deputy Field Director Christopher Pappas during party welcoming the Lieberman interns, Manchester; **p. 64-65** (l-r) Dean team's Delana Jones jostles for position with Edwards team's Megan Scott during the Manchester Mental Health fundraising walk; **pp. 66-67** David Moore, Graham HQ, Manchester; **pp. 68-69** Team Dean's Delana Jones and Nashua Regional Field Director Marc Baronov (at bat) during a softball game against Team Lieberman, Manchester; **pp. 70-71** Intercampaign karaoke competition, Manchester; **p. 72** (l-r) Karen Hicks and Senior Advisor Maura Keefe with other Dean staff and supporters en route to Howard Dean's campaign announcement event held in his hometown of Burlington, VT; **pp. 74-75** Karen Hicks (center) during Howard Dean's speech announcing his candidacy for President, Burlington, VT; **pp. 78-79** Caleb Clark (in reflection, center) waiting outside during a small meeting of Edwards' supporters, Salem; **pp. 80-81** Staff orientation, Dean HQ, Manchester; **pp. 82-83** Traveling Press Secretary Jamal Simmons speaking with Bob Graham in front of the NASCAR truck that Graham sponsored, before a live television appearance, Concord; **p. 84** Jessie Grant (r) before July 4th parade steps off, Amherst; **p. 85** Dean staffers including Emily Barson (bullhorn) march with supporters during July 4th parade, Merrimack; **p. 86** NH State Director Erik Greathouse (r) running a staff meeting to organize an upcoming candidate trip, Gephardt HQ, Manchester; **p. 88** Erik Greathouse (l), NH Deputy Field Director Geoff Ward; **p. 89** Volunteer Coordinator/Office Manager Claire Wilker (r-front) during the Nashua Pride baseball game, Hollman Stadium, Nashua; **pp. 90-91** Kristin Carvell taking an ice cream break, near the "JoeMobile" owned by her fellow Lieberman staffer, Raymond Buckley, Puritan Backroom Restaurant parking lot, Manchester; **pp. 92-93** Cheering squads during the intercampaign softball games, Manchester; **p. 94** Nick Clemons reorganizing the Kerry HQ for a campaign event featuring the candidate, Manchester; **pp. 96-97** Karen Hicks (l) leading a yoga break during a Dean staff retreat, Camp Moosilauke, Orford; **p. 98** (l-r) NH Trip Coordinator Meghan Scott, John Edwards, and NH Field Director Laura Walters during Edwards' call time, Edwards HQ, Manchester; **p. 99** Former Illinois Sen. Carol Moseley Braun meeting and talking with voters/churchgoers, New Hope Church, Portsmouth; **pp. 100-101** NH Communications Director Kathy Roeder doing final preparation for Dick Gephardt's arrival to the Teamsters' endorsement event, JFK Coliseum, Manchester; **pp. 102-103** Mike Mattoon and volunteer Sarah Greathouse (l- bottom) working with many other Gephardt staffers and supporters at the Teamsters' endorsement of Gephardt, JFK Coliseum, Manchester; **pp. 104-105** Kerry campaign staffers, including Heidi Kraus (center), and interns prepping for HQ open house, Manchester; **pp. 106-107** Sunset reflected in the windows of the Lieberman HQ, Manchester; **pp. 108-109** Screensaver showing picture from Dean's Burlington, VT announcement of his Presidential Candidacy, Dean HQ, Manchester; **p. 110** Teamsters' endorsement of Gephardt, JFK Coliseum, Manchester; **p. 111** Sign marking the route to a Dean event, Peterborough; **p. 113** NH Deputy State Director Emily Silver packing up the Lieberman campaign's JoeMobile, Cheshire County Fair, Swanzey; **pp. 114-115** Staffers from the Dean campaign preparing for, then celebrating the success of, their Dean Organizing Convention, the first coming together of their volunteer-based field organization, Center of New Hampshire, Manchester; **p. 116** Jessie Grant greeting house party attendees before Kerry's arrival, home of Alan and Joan Reische, Manchester; **p. 119** Dick Gephardt speaking to a full house during an early visit at the home of Ed and Leslee Stewart, Manchester; **pp. 120-121** John Kerry speaking to Democratic activist and former Ambassador George Bruno with Kerry's NH Political Director Theo Yedinsky following close behind, home of Alan and Joan (r) Reische, Manchester; **p. 122-123** Kathy Roeder (l) looking on as fellow staffers including Mike Mattoon cook hot dogs and hamburgers for assembled supporters shown listening to Dick Gephardt's stump speech beneath a tent at Jim Demers' family home, Dover; **p. 124** Manchester's annual Greek fall festivals offer a healthy selection of potential supporters: John Edwards (top) meeting and greeting the crowd; Howard Dean dancing to Greek music with supporters including Stanley Spirou, Manchester; **p. 125** Following closely behind their candidates: (top) Edwards NH Political Director Kristyn McLeod and NH Press Secretary Colin Van Ostern speaking with a potential supporter; (bottom) Dean campaign's Delana Jones handing out campaign literature and gathering names of potential supporters, Manchester; **p. 127** Kerry staffers Pat Morris and Andrew Stone "tabling" during the Latino Festival, downtown Manchester; **pp. 128-129** Kathy Roeder preparing the set for a Gephardt house party at the home of John and Mindy Kacavas, which was covered live by C-Span, Manchester; **p. 130** Over the course of a few weeks, the East Manchester HQ of the Graham campaign is transformed into the HQ for the Clark campaign; **pp. 132** General Wesley Clark (r) meeting and greeting voters and followed by the huge media contingent that materialized as soon as he declared his candidacy, Merrimack Restaurant, downtown Manchester; **p. 135** Lieberman staffers preparing the stage from which Lieberman would deliver a major economic policy speech, beside the Merrimack River, Manchester; **p. 136-137** Staffer Theo Yedinsky (r) lingered by John Kerry's campaign bus at the start of a firehouse "chili feed," Laconia. The events become a standard after Kerry garners the support of the firefighters union; **pp. 138-139** John Edwards making his way through the crowd after his speech to voters, with help from his staffers (l-r) Kristyn McLeod, Meghan Scott, and traveling aide Hunter Pruette, Saint Anselm College, Manchester; **pp. 140-141** Nick Clemons exchanging some last-minute thoughts with John Kerry before Kerry's stump speech begins, Jack Quigley's Pub, Portsmouth; **pp. 142-143** Peter Greenberger assessing the crowd at a town hall meeting moments before Joe Lieberman enters the room, NH Institute of Art, Manchester; **pp. 144-145** Dean campaign HQ, Manchester; **pp. 146-147** State Canvass Director Chris Smith (l) with supporters and staff listening to Wesley Clark (r) speak after filing his candidacy papers with the NH Secretary of State, State House grounds, Concord; **pp. 148-149** Howard Dean making his way through the crowd with help from his traveling aide (r-middle) Mike O'Mary, Alpine Club, Manchester's West Side; **p. 151** Volunteer Coordinator Kinsey Casey (l) and NH Constituency Organizer Pauly Rodney leading Edwards supporters in creative chanting outside the Planned Parenthood-sponsored debate, Center of New Hampshire, Manchester; **p. 153** Gephardt staffers (l-r) NH Field Director Anna Landmark, Mike Mattoon, and Claire Wilker unloading 4' x 8' signs which they then carry up to their office, downtown Manchester; **p. 154** Staffers running one of their near-nightly "house meetings" as part of the Dean innovative field plan to talk about what draws people to the Dean campaign and how to organize within communities, east Manchester; **p. 155** Dean staffer Emily Barson preparing a sign at the Dean HQ to be displayed in the visibility area during the ABC News-sponsored debate the following evening; **pp. 156-157** Edwards field staffer Katherine Miller making her way through a huge snowstorm to go door-to-door, Manchester; **pp. 158-159** Using a creative "visibility" tactic during the ABC News-sponsored debate, Durham; **p. 160** Out-of-state Clark volunteers sleeping at the YMCA, Goffstown; **pp. 162-163** Crash pad for many a Dean staffer and volunteer, especially toward the end of the campaign season. This apartment, rented by members of the Dean Campaign, is affectionately known as "The Frat," Manchester; **p. 165** After a long day at work, (l-r) Kerry staffer Theo Yedinsky with Lieberman staffers Joe Eyer, Peter Greenberger, Edwards staffer Laura Memory Walters, and Lieberman staffer Emily Silver for a drink at their favorite watering hole, the Wild Rover Pub, downtown Manchester; **pp. 166-167** Manchester's Jillian's Bar & Grill is another popular bar for staffers. Here (clockwise) Edwards staffer Kinsey Casey joins her roommate, Delana Jones. And the rest of the Dean campaign gathers to celebrate Robby Mook's birthday (l-lower) where he is presented with his likeness, Mini-Mook; **pp. 168-169** NH Deputy Press Secretary Kristina Saunders (l) and other Clark staffers working at a pancake breakfast attended by over 200 people. Both the staff and the candidate himself (r) flip flapjacks, VFW, Nashua; **p. 171** Dean's Seacoast Regional Field Organizer Ben LaBolt taking care of a few last-minute details before the town hall event begins, Town Hall, Exeter, NH; **p. 172** Kathy Roeder affixing a cordless microphone to Dick Gephardt's tie before his campaign event, which was carried live on C-Span, Manchester, NH; **p. 173** The back room at the large Kerry campaign HQ, serving as storage space for visibility materials, Manchester; **p. 174** Laptops replace notebooks for the traveling press as they cover Howard Dean on the campaign trail, Palace Theater, Manchester; **p. 177** Wesley Clark speaking to a room of supporters and curious voters, NH Charitable Foundation, Concord; **pp. 178-179** Howard Dean swarmed by media and supporters in what becomes a regular occurrence for him on the campaign trail, Executive Court Conference Center, Manchester, NH; **pp. 180-181** Dean (l) meeting the crowd after speaking to a full house at the Music Hall in Portsmouth; Senior Advisor Maura Keefe (r) helps organize the press's departure after the event ends; **pp. 182-183** The research team hard at work, Kerry HQ, Manchester; **pp. 184-185** Hillary Hampton, press intern, awaiting straggling reporters outside of Dean town hall meeting, the Music Hall, Portsmouth; **pp. 186-187** Kathy Roeder (l) reacting to the news that her candidate, Dick Gephardt, finished a disappointing fourth place in the Iowa caucuses; Supporters and staff (r) in the main room of the campaign HQ just as CNN declares Kerry the winner; **pp. 188-189** The Edwards campaign staff cheering as he gives his speech following the Iowa caucuses. Edwards finished a surprising close second to Kerry, Manchester; **pp. 190-191** The entire Manchester-based staff and many supporters including NH Volunteer Coordinator Johanna Voss, Lead Advance man Travis Dredd, and advance staffer Melanie Roe watching the Iowa results on a rented large-screen TV, Kerry HQ, Manchester; **pp. 192-193** Gephardt campaign's Kathy Roeder (l) packing up her apartment soon after the Iowa caucus because her candidate pulled out of the race, while Edwards campaign's Kinsey Casey (r) leads cheers and chants before her candidate takes the stage, Palace Theater, Manchester; **pp. 194-195** John Kerry entering a standing-room-only hall at Phillips Exeter Academy. His win in Iowa brings a great charge to his NH campaign, and crowds flock to hear him speak, Exeter; **p. 196** Satellite trucks and vans clutter the streets of downtown Manchester in the days leading up to the election; **pp. 198-199** Staff and supporters of all the campaigns outside polling sites around the state on Election Day for visibility; **pp. 200-201** Members of the Dean campaign, including Office Manager Rachel Sobelson (on telephone), Area Organizer David Gringer, and Health Care Organizer Allison Dale watching with sadness and dismay as CNN declares John Kerry the winner of the NH primary, Dean HQ, Manchester, NH; **pp. 202-203** CNN carries the speeches made by the five top candidates following their minute-by-minute coverage of Primary Day; **pp. 204-205** Total victory at the Kerry HQ, Manchester; **pp. 206-207** Dean staffers and supporters at the Election Night "celebration" site. Rachel Sobelson (r) and her father listen as Howard Dean thanks his supporters and staff, Southern New Hampshire University, Manchester, NH; **p. 208** State Director Ken Robinson (r) thanking and congratulating the team, including Theo Yedinsky (l) and Jessie Grant. Ken also announces their work assignments following the NH primary, Kerry HQ, Manchester; **p. 209** In the days that follow, some staffers stay behind to organize and clean out the massive Kerry HQ, Manchester: **pp. 210-211** Winners and losers alike have to pack up their campaign HQ, though most staff leaves town immediately following the NH election, Dean HQ, Manchester; **p. 215** Dean campaign's Karen Hicks hugging staffers Jarel LaPan and Allison Dale following Dean's speech on Election Night, Southern NH University, Manchester; **Back cover**: Kerry campaign HQ, Manchester.

ACKNOWLEDGEMENTS

The idea for this project, and its undertaking, seemed to come to us almost as second nature. Our early thoughts of the ways we might engage in the 2004 election quickly evolved into discussions of joining our two passions—documentary photography and Presidential politics. As we finalize these pages over a year later, we wish to acknowledge the many who helped us get here. From feeding us in mind and body to helping us find the project's final form, we are indebted to friends, colleagues, and even a few strangers.

Our unique access to the campaigns and to our writers would not have been possible had the national senior management not given the project their endorsement. Karen Hicks, Ken Robinson, Peter Greenberger, and Erik Greathouse were especially encouraging of their staffers and helped us gravitate to some of their most talented storytellers. Individual staffers gave enormously of themselves during a year that offered them little in the way of spare time. Ultimately, it is their voices that bring a poetic and poignant quality to the pages of *Primarily New Hampshire*. Our collaborators made us cry; they made us laugh; they changed our lives.

We are grateful to our honorable foreword writer, Bob Kerrey, whose unique sense of public service and deep love of photography helped him to understand the potential of this project instantly. Beyond sharing his words in these pages, he also arranged for generous support for the project through New School University, where he serves as president. Without his support, we could not have produced this book.

A chance meeting with Will's old friend ABC News Political Director Mark Halperin at Manchester's Back Room Restaurant eventually helped bring the project to George Stephanopoulos' Sunday morning show. We owe a special thanks to both Mark and George for recognizing the essence of the project at its very earliest stage and helping share it with their national audience.

It's important to recognize the leading ladies of New Hampshire Democratic politics. Governor Jeanne Shaheen's many years in office and her participation during this campaign season helped inspire and teach a whole new generation of young political operatives, including many of our project writers. And, of course, Democratic State Committee Chair Kathy Sullivan, who, along with the help of her hard-working staff, kept a level playing field during the primary, and continually reminded the campaigns that they all shared a common goal.

We are also grateful for those individuals who always find time in their busy lives to help people and projects they believe in. For their generosity of ideas, we'd like to thank Nick Mitropoulos, Heather Campion, Kathy McLaughlin, Stephanie Cutter, Michael Stratton, John Sasso, Dave Contarino, MJ Blanchette, Anne Botteri, Mica Stark, and Michael Wolfson. As we worked to find support for the traveling exhibition that accompanies this publication, the New Hampshire Political Library, and specifically Michael Chaney, met the challenge with a grant to help make the exhibit possible.

And to the project's godfather, Chuck Campion, we owe endless thanks. Chuck sat through our earliest slide shows and then lent his humor and good will to the project. He helped us realize our plans and directed us to the countless people he's worked with in his lifetime of dedication to the Democratic Party. He called in countless favors to ensure that this book would reach its audience. He is an inspiration to us and all his fellow campaign activists.

Our deep appreciation goes out to those who have helped and inspired us to see this through to the end: Billy, Ro, and Debbie Shore for their loving encouragement and understanding of the commitment required to produce the book; Andi Schreiber for understanding the importance of sending us pictures of her growing boys and for always taking Meryl's phone calls from the road; Paul Keefe for getting us Web-ready; Maura Keefe for her steady perspective. And a huge thanks to Flip Brophy for her early guidance. Thanks both to Susan Meiselas, for her encouragement, understanding, and great flexibility during this past year, and to Abby Heyman, who continues to inspire Meryl's love of bookmaking. To Dan Habib for loaning us his eyes and ears as we compiled the book and for helping us find the amazing Felice Belman who, along with poet/writer Margaret Muirhead, helped bring the power of the words forward and leave the typos behind.

Our young interns, Erin Johnson, who helped work through hours of audio tape, and Sara Wolf, who carried great spirit and curiosity, reminded us daily how powerful politics can be in the lives of young people. We were especially fortunate that Rachel Sobelson was able to join our team after leaving her campaign job. Rachel brings bright light and positive energy to every challenge she takes on and every room she enters.

A very special thanks to our designer, John Peters, for his calm, quiet diligence and his artful sense of page space. Thanks also to Jay Mandarino, Alan Jordan, and the rest of the CJ Graphics team for helping us through the production process and to Lesley Sparks for pointing us in their direction.

Primarily New Hampshire took over our lives during the 14 months it took to produce. Our family and friends were kind enough to give us the space we needed to focus on the tasks at hand. We hope that they will be willing to take us back, now that the project is completed. Thanks to Judy and Stan Levin for their unending enthusiasm; to Lynda Kanteres for her chicken soup and other remedies; to Rick and Maureen Loeffler for all the Sunday dinners; to Dan Calegari, Libby Birnie, and Joe and Jo-Jo Keefe for their keen sense of New Hampshire and their healthy perspective on the Presidential primary. And thanks to our so-called dog, Lefty, for adding so many campaign staffers to his herd and for keeping us company in the studio late at night.

And lastly, a nod and a wink to the special team of contributors who joined us for countless Beech Street dinners. They helped make the year in Manchester extra special for us. May our paths continue to cross.

—ML & WJK, April 2004

IN MEMORY OF
E. LEO & ZOE KANTERES.